MANAGING THE MAVERICKS

MANAGING THE MAVERICKS

KAYE THORNE

First published in 2001 by Chandos Publishing (Oxford) Limited

Revised edition first published in 2003 by
Spiro Press
17–19 Rochester Row
London SW1P 1LA
Telephone: +44 (0)870 400 1000

ISBN 1 904298 48 6

British Library Cataloguing-in-Publication Data.
A catalogue record for this book is available from the British Library.
Library of Congress Cataloging-in-Publication Data on file.

Spiro Press USA
3 Front Street
Suite 331
PO Box 338
Rollinsford NH 03869
USA

Typeset by: Turn-Around Typesetting Ltd, Maulden
Printed in Great Britain by: The Cromwell Press
Cover image by: Gettyimages
Cover design by: Cachet Creatives

This book is dedicated to all those who are passionately committed to making a difference, within their family, within their team, within their organization. May you gain the support and understanding of others, so that future generations of learners and employees may learn and work in an environment that celebrates creativity and innovation, nurtures talent and recognizes the right of every individual to fulfil their potential.

It is also dedicated in particular to all those people who responded to the Managing the Mavericks questionnaire and to the following people, who willingly gave their time to be interviewed as case studies:

Ian Banyard	Jonathan Evans
Ben and Jonathan Finn	Peter Honey
Will Keith	Llorett Kemplen
Bill Legg	Sheena Matthews
Stephanie Oerton	Andy Pellant
Graham Rawlinson	Dr Alan Stanhope

My heartfelt thanks to all of you for your wisdom, your inspiration and your openness.

Contents

Prologue

In this book there are woven a number of strands of a story…

The story begins…

Once upon a time there was a village where everyone worked for the same employer, the most influential people in the organization lived in a castle at the top of the highest hill. Although they cared for the people in the village below, their castle was watched by guards who lived halfway up the hill. They protected the people in the castle by telling them only what they thought they wanted to hear.

The guards believed that they were very wise and so every time the villagers came up with new ways of doing things the guards looked at their suggestions and shook their heads saying, 'We tried that before, it didn't work'. Meanwhile, the people in the castle shook their heads sadly as they watched their pile of gold getting smaller. They wondered why no one from their wonderful village came to see them and every time they suggested going to see the villagers the wise guards said that everything was under control and not to worry.

Meanwhile, in another part of the village, a man rode in quietly. He entered the local hostelry and started to talk to the villagers, each person he met he took to a quiet corner and asked them the same questions: 'What are you really good at?' 'If you could do anything what would it be?' 'What don't you want to do?' He never offered them anything, he never made any promises, he just asked them questions and really listened to their answers.

Whenever he came into the hostelry he always remembered them and addressed them by name. Eventually their curiosity got the better of them and they asked him what he was doing in their village. He explained that he was working on a new invention that, if he could make it work successfully, would revolutionize the way people communicated with each other. As he had been so interested in them the villagers wanted to help him and so eventually he took some of them to visit his outbuildings after they had finished working.

Fuelled by his enthusiasm, small talented groups of engineers began to find innovative ways of building his new machine. Their enthusiasm and excitement was quietly shared with others and each evening small groups of workers would leave the big office where they worked and almost run to their evening activity where there was such enthusiasm and camaraderie. The inventor took care of them; he couldn't afford to pay them much money, but he fed them, arranging the food on large community tables, and he made sure that each evening they ended with a period of reflection about what they had all achieved that evening. Every little success was shared and every frustration was highlighted together with a suggestion of how to resolve it. Over the months the new machine went through a number of development stages from initial design to prototype and testing. One day he greeted the villagers who had helped him with a broad smile, 'We have just sold our first machine!' he told them. The villagers cheered and threw their hats in the air; they were so proud and happy for the inventor. 'Now I can afford to pay you properly' he said. 'If I can sell a few more machines I could even afford to offer some of you the opportunity to come and work with me.'

He was overwhelmed by their response; they all wanted to work for him. He knew that this was a critical time, this was the moment that he feared most; he knew that his success meant that he could no longer operate on informal goodwill, he would have to become a proper company and he was worried that he would become like the men in the castle on top of the hill. All night he tossed and turned in his bed, and then just before dawn he had an idea.

That evening he called a meeting of all the villagers who had helped him to build the machine. 'Do you remember,' he said, 'when I first arrived and I asked you to share your hopes and dreams with me? I have been thinking a lot about what you said and I don't want to encourage you to leave one company and put you into another restricted situation. I want to create an experiment in a way of working where we all work towards common goals, we work together on the big project, but you can also have time to work on your own dreams.

'I won't need a castle because we are all working together; I won't need the guards as we will manage ourselves. This company will be your company; my success will be your success. I want you all to talk to our customers and I want us all to share the good times and the bad. As well as our meetings, I want us to have meetings with our customers and the people who supply us with components. As we grow I want to set up businesses like ours in other villages and we must stay close and share our story with the new people so that they feel part of us.

'I want us to celebrate sales and new inventions, but also to celebrate personal events, birthdays, anniversaries and new babies. I never want to grow so big that I can't personally welcome each new person into the company. I want you to continue to be so proud of our products and the way we work that you would want any member of your family to come and work with us.'

Meanwhile back in the castle, the leaders looked down at their village and shook their heads at the inactivity. They called a meeting of all guards, 'What is happening?' shouted the leaders, 'the gold is almost all gone, we keep hearing reports that our customers don't like what we are selling any more, and it doesn't look very busy down there, what have you done with our people?' 'We don't know,' said the guards sullenly, 'it's not our fault the customers aren't coming anymore and we can't get the right staff.'

'Well, we have to do something; put out a proclamation that we want bright, innovative people; get some consultants in; do an attitude survey of our people; send out a questionnaire to our customers – that will sort it out' agreed the leaders. Having been told what to do the guards went away happy. The consultants came in and took away most of the remaining money but six months later the castle was empty and the guards, to their surprise, found themselves looking for new jobs.

Meanwhile, in another part of the village, the rest of the villagers were working in the new enterprise where they felt their creativity and innovation were recognized and their views respected. They didn't need managing; their pride and ownership of the new company meant that they came to work inspired and full of enthusiasm, they saw any issues and problems as challenges that gave them an opportunity to work together to find a creative solution. They remembered how it used to be in the big company and wondered why the wise guards and the clever men in the castle never took the time to talk to them or listen to their ideas, or if they ever realized what talent lay undiscovered in the village.

Acknowledgements

This book reflects a passion that I have had for many years about creativity and innovation, but also reflects the excitement, the thrill and the special feeling that occurs when you meet like-minded people. Sharing ideas, talking and exploring what it is like to be a Maverick has been a very special experience and I am so grateful to all those people who were willing to talk to me about their experiences. This book is also your book, it reflects your passion, your hopes and dreams. I hope those reading it will hear and act on your wisdom.

I would also like in these acknowledgements to pay tribute to my family, friends, colleagues, clients and fellow authors to whom I owe a great debt of gratitude for their ongoing care, support and inspiration.

Kelvin Harris, Matt Thorne, Louise Thorne, Steve Bedford and the whole team at Learn 2 Earn Ltd, Chris and Vivien Dunn and the whole team at TDA Transitions Ltd, Alex Machray, David Mackey, Mark Woodhouse, John Kenney, Ian and Rosemary Anderson, Paul Allen, Kevin McGrath, Paul Ewins, Keith Harriss, Rob and Sue Ford, Margaret and Les Ellyatt, Bill and Bernice Legg, Sid and Elizabeth Cole, Eileen and Gordon Nicholls, Charles and Jean Burrows, Diana and Nigel Gray, Joy and Peter Gunson, William Henwood, Keith Bastin, Richard and Lindy Bishop, Babs Bonner, Vivien Bolton,

Margaret Cortis, Bill Eldridge, Carolin, Ross, Ben and Laura Garside, Chris George, Mark Gordon, Will and Anya Keith, Peter Lightfoot, Cheri Lofland, Philip Mudd, Chris Phelps, Sheila Rundle, Lesley Shaw, Mark Sinclair, Alan Smith, Doug and Lisa Twining, the Kilby Family.

I also want to acknowledge the work of those who created the models and concepts that underpin many creative and innovative activities, in particular: Tony Buzan for his innovative Mind Maps ® method; Peter Honey and Alan Mumford for their Learning Styles Questionnaire; David A Kolb for his Experiential Learning Model; Joseph Wallas and Jules-Henri Poincaré for their models of the Stages of Creativity; Edward de Bono's Six Thinking Hats; Howard Gardner and his description of Multiple Intelligences; Paul Torrance for his work in highlighting the importance of creativity in education. All the authors mentioned in the bibliography. All the staff at the CIPD and IOD libraries for their help in compiling the bibliography. Anne Rees for all her dedication in making sense of the book.

Finally, all the very special clients and individual learners who ultimately have been my inspiration.

My grateful thanks to you all.

Introduction

In his 1997 book, *The Circle of Innovation*, Tom Peters asked the following question:

'Why are there so f-e-w books... on INNOVATION... and s-o-o-o many on teams/empowerment/re-engineering/quality? (1) Beats me! (2) Too hard?'

I would like to add a second observation; why, even in the books that *are* written, is so much duplicated? This is not a criticism of my fellow authors, but is from a sense of frustration that we have made such little progress in understanding what is such a fundamental part of our lives.

In this book I have tried to redress part of this imbalance. As well as researching the traditional views, definitions and theories of creativity and innovation, I have also spent time interviewing and conducting a survey (2001) with individuals who identified themselves as being creative and innovative, or who could be described as 'Maverick'.

As part of my background research I had a letter published in *People Management*, a leading UK Human Resources magazine, inviting people to contact me if they would describe themselves as Maverick. What became very special for me as the emails came through was the willingness of people to take part, the thoughtfulness of their responses and the commitment to send the questionnaire on to others in their network, not just as a questionnaire but often with a personal endorsement. Many people showed genuine interest and encouragement in the whole process. This happened on a global basis, from the UK to the US through to India and Australia. Although the number of responses was not statistically significant, the results were nonetheless revealing.

The questionnaire invited these 'Mavericks' to identify the issues, the opportunities and the cultures that help them to develop their individual creativity and enable organizations to innovate. Their responses are analyzed in depth throughout this book and the questionnaire is reproduced in full in the Appendix.

The questionnaires are non-attributed, but another group of named individuals agreed to be interviewed as case studies (see Chapter 9).

The responses of both groups give us a privileged insight; their candour, comments, challenges and questions offer a richness of observation which uniquely takes us close to their day-to-day reality of trying to do things differently. There is valuable advice for organizations, and for CEOs and line managers, on how to both encourage, and channel, the creativity of Mavericks. There is also some advice for Mavericks themselves. Finally, there are some very poignant statements about some of the challenges faced by individuals in making personal choices about whether to stay with or leave an organization; or to have the courage to believe in themselves enough to do what they really wanted to do. This was balanced against the independence and freedom felt by those who were working for themselves.

These are people with a very different outlook on life – call them Mavericks, call them innovative, there isn't really an appropriate label that sums them up. My belief is that every individual is unique, but added to this uniqueness there are some people who are living with something else that presents them and the people or organizations with whom they interact with the opportunity to make a real difference in this world. Their responses provide some fresh insights, wisdom and another level of input into the ongoing challenge of raising the awareness and recognition of the importance of creativity and innovation as one of the key foundation stones of organizational development. They also highlight the implications for managing innovation; the need to nurture and channel creativity, to help evaluate and identify the ideas with real potential, and how to take an idea from origination through to successful implementation.

Doing things differently is not easy; challenging long-held assumptions can isolate individuals. Equally, there is also the need, as many of the Mavericks themselves will acknowledge, to provide checks and balances. Sometimes Maverick behaviour can be seen as high risk, however, with the creation of an open environment, organizations can develop a platform for support and positive challenge where ideas can be evaluated and risks fully explored.

Will you make a difference?

The reason why I wrote this book, and why I believe everyone so willingly took the time to complete the questionnaire and take part in the case studies, is that we care, not just mildly, but passionately about people, the environment they work and learn in and the right of every individual to fulfil their potential.

What perplexes us is why some of the most blindingly simple strategies aren't in place to achieve this. Every comment made, every question asked is within the remit and power of most CEOs, executive boards and organization leaders. Most suggestions are linked to attitude and behaviour, so the cost implications to the bottom line are negligible; in terms of human capital the reward would be high.

We are not alone in our passion, some of the world's greatest leaders have already demonstrated that managing Mavericks effectively brings business success, but nothing will change until enough individuals with power and persuasion decide to make a real difference.

We all have choices; leaders can choose whether they are really committed to leading, inspiring and caring about their people. Organizations can choose to come alive, recognize the real needs of their employees and set them free to contribute to the lifeblood of the organization. Individually we choose whether to share what we know and help energize others; whether to give or to take.

Just imagine if leaders, organizations and individuals took seriously the need to *really* work together – what a difference that would make.

Writing this book has been like constructing an orchestral score with input from many talented musicians. I owe an enormous debt of gratitude to everyone who took part. Each person gave me their own particular combination of notes which, when added to mine, created a harmony that was so much more inspiring than anything I could have created on my own.

I hope you will enjoy listening to the music and that it will inspire you to experiment and improvize in your lives and workplaces.

CHAPTER 1

Defining innovation

Setting the scene

Defining innovation is not a simple task, it is much more than a simple dictionary definition; by its very nature it goes to the heart of an organization. The act of innovating involves more than just a creative thought; to be successful it needs emotional competencies such as self-confidence, persistence and the ability to influence and persuade. It also needs commercial awareness. As mentioned in the Introduction, there are comparatively few books about innovation, but the quotes below are taken from a selection of other writers and leaders who illustrate the importance of doing it differently.

Innovation is not neat

'Never try to control, or make safe the fumbling, panicky, glorious and chaotic adventure of discovery. Occasionally I see articles that describe how to rationalize the invention process, how to take the fuzzy front end and give it a nice haircut... I would urge you to make that fuzzy front end as unkempt and as furry as you can because innovation is not neat. We stumble on many of our best discoveries. If you want to follow the rapidly moving leading edge you have to learn to live on your feet; you must be willing to make those necessary healthy stumbles.'

William Coyne,
Senior Vice President Research & Development, 3M

Creativity does not necessarily come in tidy packages

'The creative mind is by its very nature, a bit unruly. There is a natural tension between orderly self-control and innovative urge. It's not that people who are creative are out-of-control emotionally; rather, they are willing to entertain a wider range of impulse and action than do less adventurous spirits. That is after all, what creates new possibilities.'

Daniel Goleman, *Working with Emotional Intelligence*

Organizations need to challenge the status quo

'To succeed, we must stop being so goddam normal. If we behave like all the others, we will see the same things, come up with similar ideas, and develop identical products or services. At its best, normal output will produce normal results. In a winner takes all world, normal = nothing. But, if we are willing to take one little risk, break one tiny rule, disregard a few of the norms, there is at least a theoretical chance that we will come up with something different, actually get a niche, create a short-term monopoly, and make a little money. Funky business is like playing the lottery. If you participate, there is a 99% chance that you will lose. On the other hand if you do not take part, your chances of losing are 100%.'

Ridderstråle and Nordstrom, *Funky Business*

We need people who are different

'We have been given a gift. In my dad's time the message was, "Hunker down, keep your nose clean; don't make waves"... It was the right message that he passed to me in 1957... It's exactly the wrong message now... And the question is: Will we live up to the (insane) times? That is will you/me/we use the gift we have been given... or squander it?... Will we have the guts, the nerve, the persistence, the PASSION to live our life as loudly as these very loud times demand? For your and my careers, for our units, for our organizations, for our families, for our communities, for our nation... it's the $64 trillion question. So...? LIVE LOUD.'

Tom Peters, *The Circle of Innovation*

We need to break out... be free

'Companies that shun creative risks may be undercut by competitors not only with products and services, but also with better processes and ways of perceiving new opportunities. Escaping the stagnation of the *status quo*, of the risk-free life, is part of the exhilaration of jamming in music and in business. The choice is stark, create, or fail.'

John Kao,
Jamming: The Art & Discipline of Business Creativity

So what can we learn from the above? Let's highlight some of the key words:

PANICKY – GLORIOUS – CHAOTIC – FUZZY – STUMBLE
UNRULY – IMPULSE – ADVENTURE – RISK – FUNKY
LOSE – ESCAPING STAGNATION – EXHILARATION –
JAMMING – INSANE – GUTS – NERVE – PERSISTENCE –
PASSION – LIVE LOUD

Not necessarily the words that most people in the corporate world feel comfortable with, and yet all the research into creativity and innovation shows that it is not a tidy, ordered science; from failure may eventually come success.

It does involve energy, passion, raw nerve, guts and often frustration, anger and exhaustion, and yet it is all worth it for the glorious heady moments of inspiration and success.

Organizations that allow risk-taking often benefit from improved motivation, enhanced customer service and idea generation. CEOs that listen to their people often find out more about their corporate climate than those who shut themselves away. Throwing away the corporate rule book that says 'this is the way we do things around here' and creating an environment of trust, respect and empathy does not mean anarchy rules. What it can do instead is create an environment where individuals feel confident to make suggestions and where the line management, and ultimately the organization itself, feeds on its own creativity and innovation. It is far easier to say 'No' than it is to say 'Let's try it and see'; the former is final, the latter involves the threat of change and experimentation, which can make traditionalists feel uncomfortable. It can also imply that instead of sending someone away to continue doing what they have always done, individuals have to take responsibility for that change. With this may come a threat of failure, and many individuals in organizations would rather stay with what is known and comfortable than risk the unknown.

One of the most famous examples of innovation is the 3M 15% policy, which allowed employees time to work on their own projects and resulted in the development of the Post-it® note. Almost everyone reading about innovation will come across this example, but the fact that you read about it so often reinforces the point mentioned in the Introduction to this book: there are comparatively few other examples of this occurring.

One of the most important and salutary lessons from this is to help organizations recognize the importance of innovating, accelerating and innovating again. Both the Fortune and FTSE Top 100 companies bear evidence of the great blue chip companies who have exited over the last 20 years to be replaced by organizations that realize the importance of continuous innovation. There is an example of this in Tom Peters' book *The Circle of Innovation* where he refers to the work of Jim Utterback, author of *Mastering the Dynamics of Innovation*:

> 'Time after time the industry leaders react to the threat of change by polishing yesterday's apple'.

It is such a powerful analogy: organizations cannot afford just to look at their existing fruit bowl. They need to be recruiting and retaining talent. They need to be creating environments where it is a virtue to be different. However, they also need to be continuously improving what already exists and monitoring their service levels. In practice, this will mean giving individuals permission to be brilliant, to share their enthusiasm for new product development, and encouraging their consumers not just to tell them what is wrong with their service, but actually to work alongside them, listening to their wants and needs.

One of the key factors in the exponential growth of e-commerce in the late 1990s was the impact of creative and entrepreneurial young people who saw the growth of web-based industry as an opportunity not only to make money, but also to create their own working environments and take control of their own destiny. E-commerce was described as the new rock and roll, yet we all know that the most successful and enduring rock bands needed both their musical talent and sound business advice to survive. The same is true of the dot.coms. Those that have survived have had to learn the lessons of how to run a successful business; the technology gave them different access to their customers, but the business principles still needed to be applied. Today's young entrepreneurs need to recognize the same issues, they need to back up their energy and creativity with sound infrastructures.

Retaining talent is critical in today's economic environment; every employer needs to identify why their employees would want to stay with them. What is your organization offering the Mavericks? However we try to disguise it, people who are creative *are* different. In my research with people who described themselves as Mavericks there was a clear recognition of the implications of their overwhelming need to do things differently (see chapters 4 and 9).

It is often difficult to apply order to creativity; these individuals have also had a lifetime of asking questions, or making suggestions that may have been largely ignored or dismissed as being either too fanciful, impractical, or too difficult to answer. The reasons for this are many, the ability to be creative and to generate innovative ideas has often been perceived as something outside the normal realm of behaviour. Inventors like Trevor Baylis (of clockwork radio fame), James Dyson (vacuum cleaners) and Steve Jobs of Apple are often viewed with a mixture of awe and scepticism and in many ways creative people often suffer for their craft before they gain recognition, particularly if they challenge assumptions or the *status quo*.

Generating ideas and being innovative takes tremendous personal discipline; every person who is creative lives with the pressure of days when their mind is a complete blank, and they often have the additional pressure of knowing that their manager or team is waiting for them to come up with original thoughts. Equally, they know that when they leave work, and are at home at night, they may suddenly find their mind racing with the solution to the problem they have been wrestling with all day. Allowing people to take time out to think or to create their own personal space is essential for the development of creativity. Often it only takes a small adjustment in the management process to allow the degree of flexibility that creative people crave.

Managing the process of innovation is absolutely critical for its success. Understanding how ideas are generated, sponsoring creative thinkers and allowing people the freedom to think is an important part of the role of any manager. This support also needs to include opportunities for real and constructive feedback. The process has to include testing and piloting to identify what works, what needs modification and what may need further research. The really excellent managers are those who assemble teams where creative and innovative people are supported by others who can help them explore their ideas and can help them take the idea to the next stage of making it happen. Within this environment high trust develops, allowing ideas to be challenged, modified and implemented while remaining true to the original concept, thus enabling the creative and innovative people to move on to generating the next good idea.

Some definitions

An equal challenge is trying to define creativity, innovation and Mavericks. For the purposes of this book I would like to explore the following definitions taken in the context of building a prototype of a new aircraft. (The words in brackets are taken from the *Concise Oxford Dictionary*, 9th edition.)

Creativity: the original thought, the spark, the ignition, the original design concepts, the blueprint.
(*Inventive and imaginative, creating or able to create.*)

Without creativity, we have no real innovation; we need people who are pure idea generators, we need others who can modify those ideas. We need people who learn from others' mistakes. We need people who instead of asking 'why', ask 'why not?' or 'what if'. We need people who are capable of thinking crazy, out of the box thoughts; we need people who shake us out of complacency.

Innovation: putting that thought into practice, the engineering, the engine, the juice, the design of the chassis and build. (*Bring in new methods, ideas, make changes.*)

Innovation is not a precise, sterile activity; we need to involve our emotions, we need to challenge positively, we need to embrace the process. We need to sustain and champion a number of ideas through an evaluative process, knowing that many of them will fail, but through their failure we will find the idea that is really capable of competitive success. We need to use people with different competencies, who can move through from idea generation to implementation.

Maverick: the test pilot, the person who tries it first, the 'who dares wins', the risk taker, who gives feedback on how to improve, who is prepared to push it that little bit further, who through their own pushing may find another way of doing it. Not afraid to challenge, not necessarily respectful of authority. (*An unorthodox or independent-minded person named after Sam Maverick, Texas engineer and rancher d.1870 who did not brand his cattle.*)

We need people with the passion to embrace innovation, to be the first to try a new idea or concept, who are prepared to be the champion, even if it is untested. We want people who have the power of their convictions. The reason why test pilots may die in testing, apart from engineering faults, is the reason for the downfall of some Mavericks: which is that their risk awareness and risk management may be out of alignment. All test pilots would be aware of the risks involved, but for some they push the risk that little bit further. In their personal desire to succeed, adrenaline takes over, sometimes with tragic circumstances.

This analogy often spills over into organizations or life. Some people really do live on the edge and sometimes, as a result of their inability to control themselves or behaviours, they self-destruct, have to leave or are forced out. Every day, Mavericks are making choices – do I go, or do I stay? If I stay what are the personal implications of my decision? However, if organizations were less risk-averse more Mavericks and their talent would stay.

So how do you really encourage innovation?

One of the most over-used words in corporate communications is 'innovation'. It is found in mission and value statements, in employee competencies and inevitably in recruitment advertisements. However, the desire to acquire it often outweighs the understanding of exactly how to achieve it.

All the research in the public domain indicates the same key points; one of the fascinating facts about creativity and innovation is that if you ask any CEO about their relative importance within their organization they will all agree that they are important. However, if you subsequently ask them what they are doing about it their response is more guarded. The real issue is that although everyone wants it they really are not sure how to go about achieving it.

Organizationally the issue is even greater; there are often unnecessary barriers created between those who are perceived as 'creative' and those who are seen as more pragmatic. The really innovative organizations are those where creativity and innovation are recognized and encouraged, not in a special group of people called 'creatives' but where everyone is involved in the 'good idea' philosophy. In reality, the successful implementation of innovation needs combinations of people who have preferences in the different stages of the process (see overleaf – the Innovation 3® six-stage model of innovation).

The Innovation 3® six-stage model of innovation

Creating the climate

If the organization does not encourage and foster innovation it is unlikely that creative and innovative individuals will feel able to make a full contribution. Equally, any sources of good ideas and positive suggestions for improvement may get stifled.

Idea generation

Ideas evolve, they develop if nurtured. As well as encouraging individuals to think creatively, organizations can create processes for idea generation and business improvement.

Developing and exploring ideas

Once an idea has been generated, it needs to be taken into an 'incubation' stage where more people become involved and the idea is developed further.

Evaluation options and decision making

Sharing concepts and ideas needs to be carefully planned, but it is also important to foster an environment that encourages experiment and allows ideas to be evaluated non-judgementally (though not non-critically).

Making it happen, implementing innovation

The handover at this stage is critical, other teams may be involved. It means moving from the dream to reality.

Measuring success, monitoring innovation

It is very easy to ignore this important stage in the process, but without measurement and review the valuable lessons that could be learned will be lost, or ignored.

The challenge for organizations

One of the real challenges for an organization is how to stay ahead of the competition; in today's environment it is not enough simply to be innovative. Innovative organizations do not stand still, they understand the importance of recognizing the different stages in the innovation process and creating teams of people able to respond to the different skill sets required in the development and implementation of innovative ideas.

Instead of waiting for others to catch up they are already moving ahead in the next phase of their development. Recruiting and retaining talented people who are able to provide the creative impetus to do things differently is another challenge. These people normally adopt unorthodox ways of making things happen and they play the corporate game by their own rules. They can be like quicksilver, moving in and out of organizations with breathtaking speed.

In today's corporate environments there is real uncertainty about the future; as a result many acknowledge the need to do things differently. But while CEOs and executives may recognize the need to change, there is little guidance in how to achieve it. What is even more important is how the new CEOs appointed to bring about change are supported. So often they are charged with turning the organization around and given the very same team who are resisting the change. While organizations may talk about wanting more innovation and creativity, very few are really committed to providing the climate to support it.

The businesses that will succeed in the 21st century will recognize that there is a need to do things differently. Harnessing each individual's creativity and imagination and encouraging innovation is becoming an increasingly important focus for corporate organizations. Books like *Maverick* by Ricardo Semler, once seen as perhaps a quirky approach to organizational development (particularly in the way he changed his working relationship with his employees, see p. 21) are now seen as an important stage in a passage towards doing it differently. Value-based leadership, emotional intelligence, synchronicity and intuition are no longer seen as being outside the corporate agenda, but are understood to be an important part of individual and organizational development. Senior management are recognizing that their talent bank will be greatly depleted if they do not help people fulfil their potential.

How can organizations provide an environment that champions people who think differently? One way of doing this is by focusing on the messages that you give to your prospective employees through your advertising, recruitment information, current employees and your approach to customers. Every day corporate messages are being transmitted (often unwittingly) about how the organization conducts its business. If an organization wishes to attract creative and innovative people, in fact any employee, it needs to consider the brand messages that it is giving to those people.

True competitive edge will be achieved by those organizations that are able to attract and retain employees and that build customer loyalty through the clear transmission of the overall brand. They will be the success stories of the 21st century.

Developing an employer brand

'Branding' as a generic term is often assumed to belong to the marketing function. However, increasingly organizations are realizing that, directly or indirectly, most brand promises are delivered by people not products. Pick up any business magazine that talks about 'branding' and it is likely that they will be discussing the broader aspect of organizational, corporate or employer branding. There is also increasing emphasis on becoming an 'employer of choice'.

What is interesting is how this type of branding is defined: terms like 'corporate branding', 'organizations as brands', or more recently 'employer branding', are different descriptors of basically the same process. What is clearly being recognized is that having strong consumer brands is not enough, organizations need to broaden their focus to consider other aspects such as:

- People

- Products/services

- Processes/systems

- Premises/environment.

'Branding' an organization means focusing on the key components and encouraging consistency across all functions. Like any piece of machinery, one part cannot operate without the other. Cross-functional working breaks down the traditional divisions between marketing, sales, distribution, manufacturing and HR.

The process links new service/product development and the development of employees. It links the distribution chain with the customer. It builds relationships, not just agreements, with external suppliers. It takes the most senior managers and involves them in the front line of the business. It puts the customer in the centre and heart of the organization and builds everything else around them.

The organization doesn't just service its customers; they become its lifeblood. People do not just make promises, they deliver, not once but over and over again, consistently developing better and better service. The organization differentiates itself in the marketplace through its people, its products, its processes and its premises.

Experience has shown that in order to develop an employer/ organization brand it is important to articulate the image and vision of the future and to invite all employees to unite behind it.

This 'branding' process normally has a number of components:

Our vision (where we want to be)

This must be a real statement that people can easily remember and identify with, not just words on a wall.

Our values (what we stand for/our integrity)

If these are not daily demonstrated behaviourally by everyone in the organization they are worthless.

Standards and practices (what we demonstrate daily)

This is the way we do things, the way our performance is measured; it applies to everyone and ensures consistency.

Working in partnership (the way forward)

No person or organization can function for long alone. Working with people, helping others to be successful, building pride, self-esteem and sharing success are all important components. Equally, building close links with suppliers, encouraging the media with positive news and building links with your local community are positive partnership actions.

Showing our competitors (best practice)

Be proud of your achievements, and demonstrate best practice. Be the organization that others benchmark against. This will have internal spin-offs for morale.

Measuring our success (real measures that everyone recognizes)

Never forget where you started, realize how much progress has been made.

Rewarding performance (based on success)

Not just with money, but personal recognition, ie by regularly giving valued feedback to individuals on their actions and achievements, and reinforcing positive behaviours.

Measuring performance (be realistic)

Not 'we promise to do our best', but ' we promise to respond within 14 days, on time, and to meet identified standards'.

Giving and receiving feedback (positive and constructive)

From the bottom to the top of the organization (and *vice versa*) open up channels of communication.

Review and progress (continuously improving)

Ask 'What have we learnt?' 'Where can we innovate?'

To prevent a distorted view of the organization the process should be seamless from the front to back and top to bottom of the organization.

When asked to describe the brand of the organization, there should be a common belief based on shared vision, goals, aspirations, behaviour and practice. Everyone who is touched by your organization brand should share these common perceptions. Importantly, this is not just an internal process. In the broader context of employer branding it means the way organizations position themselves externally as well as internally. This will have a particular relevance in the way organizations promote themselves in the recruitment marketplace, or in supplier contacts.

The most fundamental part of the process is built on behaviours, based on self-esteem, confidence and pride in the organization. People must take responsibility for meeting challenges and providing innovative and creative solutions to problems. They will then rise above the mundane and gain tremendous personal and team satisfaction from providing excellent customer service.

These concepts are not fundamentally new, what is different is gaining senior level commitment and linking all the stages together in a holistic way. By bringing all the initiatives together under an organization's 'brand concept', not only is there more coherence, there's a constant benchmark. All employees should ask the question, 'Does this action, this behaviour, this response really reflect the brand?' and in doing so they create an organizational conscience so powerful that organizational success has to follow.

A strong brand image is as relevant to an organization as it is to a product or service. The people behind the product have to be consistent with the brand, and the commitment has to be reflected from the top of the organization to the newest recruit.

When people genuinely care for each other, when job applicants identify you as a preferred employer, you can see the pride and the self-esteem, you know you have developed a strong corporate brand; even more importantly, you know you have found the heart of your organization.

Finally, to quote Ricardo Semler in *Maverick*:

> 'To survive in modern times, a company must have an organizational structure that accepts change as its basic premise, lets tribal customs thrive and fosters a power that is derived from respect, not rules. In other words, the successful companies will be the ones that put quality of life first. Do this and the rest, quality of product, productivity of workers, profits for all – will follow.'

CHAPTER 2

Living outside the box

Doing it differently

A recurring theme in this book is 'doing it differently', yet that in itself is often a major issue for organizations. Creative and innovative people often find it difficult to conform, and the majority of organizations find it difficult to deal with non-conformity. One major issue is about how and when creativity may be released; for many this is almost a daily challenge.

Creative thinking is that ability to rise above the immediacy of the situation and to spot development potential, or to see linkages between different projects and to weave them together into a coherent whole.

Celebrate the difference

People find that the joy of discovery is often tempered by a dawning realization that they have to convince others that their idea is really worth investment. Creative people are sometimes perceived as somehow not quite 'grown up'. Ideas have to be 'positioned' for the organization, or senior people.

One of the difficulties creative people sometimes experience is having to explain to others their thought processes. If your mind naturally moves forward very quickly and synergistically, trying to explain to someone how you reached your conclusions can not only be frustrating but also quite difficult because you may not actually remember the specific detail of the linkages. Pushing the boundaries of creativity and innovation requires an understanding of how people learn, how people innovate and how the innovation process works within organizations.

One of the questions asked in the case study interviews was 'When did you first realize that you were different?' Several individuals were aware of this from a young age and the discovery of difference was often a positive experience. But what was fascinating in the responses was the fact that many people could remember the moment, the situation, or a feeling of being different. How this difference manifested itself was obviously personal to each individual, but in terms of timing, there were some similarities: for several it occurred in childhood, perhaps at school, or the arrival of a sibling, parents moving house – the need to go to a different school; being encouraged to perform in front of others, being made to feel special, given recognition. Sometimes the difference resulted in a self-challenge to drive for success, or to do something differently. In most cases, however, the trigger usually lay within the individual.

Being different brings with it expectations both personally and from others. It can also sometimes bring exclusion, their very difference creating discomfort with others who cannot quite comprehend the driving need to do things differently. This may be because the driver is to make a real difference and others may lack the depth of passion or commitment to want to make things happen differently. It may be that they have been charged with changing the organization and as a result others feel slightly threatened by them.

It may be because the individual decides not to share their planned actions with others; this may occur for a variety of reasons:

- The action may occur spontaneously, in response to the circumstances.

- They may believe that others will try and persuade them not to do it.

- They are still thinking their proposed action through and they are not ready to share; creative and innovative people often do need time to think. Thomas Edison, who was totally deaf in one ear and only had 10% hearing in the other ear, declared that it was not a 'handicap' but more an advantage as it gave him more time to think because he did not have to listen to small talk.

Almost every case study interviewee describes periods of time when they set themselves challenges, wanted to achieve something and as a result drove themselves to achieve it. They often do not see risk in the same way as others: they see it as something to be overcome when it happens rather than being risk-averse. That does not mean that they rush foolishly into untested situations, they will weigh up the pros and cons but will not be afraid to try something different.

Competitiveness sometimes features too, wanting to be the best, finding themselves first, gaining success, reinforcing self-belief that they can achieve what they set out to achieve.

One of the very real issues for creative and innovative people is managing their creativity in the context of what others might perceive as normal life, so that they can pursue what they want to do most… which is to 'create'.

The issues that stop creative people from fulfilling their potential are many and varied, eg:

- Having to stop working on something that is stimulating and exciting because they are told that it is not in the business plan.

- Having to stop because they need to go to a meeting that someone else has called.

- Having to stop because they have line responsibility for others who want some of their time.

- Having to stop because they are over-committed.

- Having to stop because their client, manager or team wants something from them.

- Having to stop because the funding runs out and they can't convince others of the viability of the idea.

- Having to stop because they need to convince, influence or persuade others that what they are doing is worthwhile.

- Having to stop because they need more time, energy, or resources, in short they need to eat, drink and sleep!

Organizationally the issues are very similar; creative start-up businesses are often perceived as risky. Entrepreneurial owners have many of the same issues as creative individuals within organizations. This often manifests itself when individuals leave organizations to set up on their own. Raising money and putting in management structures to run a business are time-consuming for the individual who is also trying to create and develop a business idea.

One of the real difficulties is that neither side really understands the other, and consequently each talks to the other in language that neither appreciates. This is reflected in Bennis and Biederman's study of Great Groups in *Organizing Genius,* in which they make some very important points about talented individuals and organizations. 'In Great Groups the right person has the right job... Successful leaders strip the workplace of non-essentials. Great Groups are never places where memos are the primary form of communication'. (See Chapter 4.)

If you have what you believe is a really good idea you cannot necessarily understand why someone won't fund it. If you have no experience in running a business you may not be aware of the 'burn rate' in the costs of employees, lawyers, marketing and other professionals in the setting up of a business. Identifying how much it costs to bring a great idea to market is frustrating for both the person with the great idea and the backer trying to fund it; it often revolves around something that may initially be unquantifiable. This is why the concept of 'incubators' is so attractive: they are a place where small businesses and individuals can grow while being protected by either a parent company, or a 'host' organization.

Starting from scratch is expensive; being part of an incubator is safer and ultimately may be more financially rewarding for both sides. However, incubators are still a comparatively new concept, although Ricardo Semler in his book *Maverick* also describes an innovative approach in the relationship that he had with his workers. He owns Semco, a Brazilian manufacturing company. When he took over the company he realized that he had to make radical changes, although many of the changes evolved over time. He became the questioner, the challenger and the catalyst for change. However, what is probably most significant for others seeking to learn from his experience, is the way that he changed the relationship between the organization and the employees.

Semco evolved from a paternalistic command-orientated management style to a highly democratic participative management structure. Some of the more innovative initiatives were: employees being allowed to set their hours and salary; widespread profit sharing; hiring and firing managers by employees; and individuals working to stay employed by adding visible value so that their team would want to continue to keep them in their six-month budget. Much of this was achieved by his factories and business units becoming separate self-regulating units where, as Semler suggests, 'the standard policy was no policy'.

Knowing yourself, knowing others

The biggest challenge for organizations is helping individuals to handle and respect differences. As individuals we are complex: think about your body, think about your brain, identify your learning style, think about how you prefer to work in a team. If you explore all these aspects, what you create is a complex map of your preferences and what is striking and illuminating about this is the more detailed and accurate your matrix of preferences the better able you are to work to create an environment that really works for you.

The implications of this are that the better individuals understand themselves, the better they are able to meet and respond to their needs. Each individual learner is different, recognizing these differences is an important part of coaching and helping others to learn. What is fascinating is recognizing how subtle these differences are. No two people will have exactly the same combination, and in this context we should never make broad assumptions about different learners.

We need to get underneath any system of classification and focus in much more detail on the individual and their uniqueness. The top-line results can be a useful starting point, but we need to spend time helping the individual gain a more holistic view of themselves and to use that initial understanding as a basic template on which to build. It can also help to use this information to compare and contrast results, and to identify similarities and complementary preferences with colleagues and other team members.

Therefore, as a starting point in discovering your own creativity, or that of others, examine the results of any inventories, preference tools and psychometric tests. Spend time identifying the highlights and question the results. Try to identify similar responses and outcomes. Ask probing questions to help the learner own and recognize what is important for them in the way that they learn or interact with others. Use these results too as a basis for establishing how you and others should work together. Identify how you can build on your preferences in the way that you learn or develop new skills. See each part of your profile as a building block in the foundations of your development. Recognize that the better you know yourself the better able you will be to develop new skills and insights in the future.

People often question why they should undertake psychometric tests and often see them as tools used by the organization to assess them. However, if the results are owned by the individual they can gain a greater insight into how to create an environment that works for them. Psychometric tools shouldn't be seen as tools for the organization but rather as an insight for the individual. The more you know about who you are the better able you are to predict how you will be.

With this knowledge you can move through life with a much greater understanding of what you need to perform at your best. This can be fine tuned the more you know: for example, if I have to attend a team meeting to give feedback on a creative process that I have been undertaking, there are some specific actions that I could undertake to help me get my message across clearly. These actions would be different for each individual depending on their individual profile.

Despite recognizing the importance of coaching, very few organizations have adopted a coaching culture. Understanding how ideas are generated, sponsoring creative thinkers and allowing people freedom to think are important parts of the role of any manager. One of the key steps in the management of creativity and innovation is understanding both the process and the needs of creative people.

In world-class organizations, the focus has shifted from process development to people development, and in this context, working one-to-one, developing effective coaching and mentoring and having positive and motivational conversations with people may have more impact than any other training intervention. When people genuinely care for each other and about their organization you can feel the pulse, you can see the pride and self-esteem and you know why it is important to 'do it differently'.

Sharing in each other's development is very special; making connections, delighting in the achievement of the goals and ambitions of others is still comparatively rare. Organizations often encourage individuals to compete with each other. Middle management has a critical role to play and may sometimes be more concerned with protecting their own assets than sponsoring the good ideas from their teams. Unfortunately, this happens in too many organizations (Llorett Kemplen and Bill Legg both cited this in their case studies: see Chapter 9).

Generating new ideas and being innovative takes tremendous personal discipline; every person labelled 'creative' lives with the pressure of days where their mind is a complete blank. As well as their own frustration, they may also be living with the expectation from their manager or team, or even the organization, that they have the ability to 'create' something special.

There are many studies illustrating the importance of giving effective feedback, yet in schools, at work and even in the family we rarely give individuals what they need to develop their full potential.

This is illustrated by Shad Helmstetter in *What to Say When You Talk to Yourself*, where he argues powerfully that we need to programme our brains into positive thoughts rather than the negative messages we receive in our lives. He says that leading behavioural researchers have told us that as much as '77% of everything we think is negative and counterproductive and works against us'. He then asks,

> 'What if each and every day, from the time you were a small child, you had been given an extra helping of self-confidence, double the amount of determination, and twice the amount of

belief in the outcome, what goals could you reach? Could it be that those who appear to be "luckier" than the rest have only gotten a little better programming? It is no longer a success theory. The brain simply believes what you tell it most.'

Although this has relevance for every individual it has particular relevance for creative and innovative people. In the questionnaire responses and case studies there are many poignant statements about the level of feedback that individuals want (see chapters 4, 5, 7 and 9).

The implications for organizations and individuals

Being different has huge implications for any individual, whether the difference is one of gender, ethnicity, disablement or ability. Importantly, this is not about putting everyone together into one box labelled 'different'. In fact it is exactly the opposite. It is about a mature recognition that we need to respect individual differences. However, organizations in general are not good at respecting difference, and there are few that really celebrate it. The implications for individuals who are trying to do things differently are how to share their thoughts and ideas with either their colleagues, their manager, or the organization.

This often leads to them identifying with the statement 'Fools, can't you see?' (see Chapter 3). Sharing creative ideas can be difficult because the idea generator may not know where the idea came from. Much idea generation is spontaneous. There is the well-known quote from Thomas Edison, one of the most prolific inventors, 'Genius is 1% inspiration, 99% perspiration'. In that very spontaneity there is also the issue of explaining it to others, trying to identify which idea is worth pursuing, how to move from the dream to the reality of implementation and the need to work with others to make it happen. This process is highlighted in more detail in Chapter 6.

This is often one of the major issues; many creative individuals prefer to work on their own. In the survey, when answering questions about managing others very few people wanted to do it and those who did preferred to coach rather than manage (see Chapter 4).

Why can't you be like everyone else?

> 'The easy way out is to follow the crowd, forget your ideas and be like everyone else. But to choose this path is to believe that someone else's opinion of you is more important than your opinion of yourself.'

Michael LeBoeuf, *Creative Thinking*

Tom Peters, in his book *A Passion for Excellence*, was one of the first people to introduce the power of engaging people's hearts and minds. Books like *Emotional Intelligence* by Daniel Goleman, Peter Senge's *Fifth Discipline* and Jaworski's *Synchronicity: The Inner Path of Leadership*, highlight a growing shift in organizations towards a recognition that there is more to business success than systems and processes. More and more people are recognizing that organizational cultures are changing, if you aspire to be world class it is important to explore these changes. Many organizations now have the word passion in their mission or vision statements. Values-based leadership is on boardroom agendas. However, examples of the concepts being demonstrated in practice are rare, which represents both a challenge and an opportunity for organizations and individuals.

If you want to explore your own feelings, or help others explore and develop new skills, then personal growth and exploration should be part of your own development agenda. Exploring different forms of motivation, thinking outside traditional forms of training and development, and pushing the boundaries of your own experience will help you develop the sensitivity that is required in taking individuals outside their comfort zone. By this I do not mean exposing individuals to situations that are dangerous, or exploitative, but instead providing a safe and supportive environment which helps people to grow and develop in ways they may not have believed possible.

Inspiring others

If your goal is to be inspiring then a good place to start is to think about what inspires you. Think back over your career, who stands out as an inspirational teacher, lecturer or manager? The person, or people who have been significant in helping us learn are often unsung, but fondly remembered. They stand out for their qualities of interest, creativity, energy, support and feedback. Think about the people you have worked with, what was it about their style that inspired you? What did you do differently as a result? By reviewing your own performance you can begin to identify your own effectiveness. The better you know yourself, the more objective you can be, and the better able you are to undertake self-assessment.

Doing it differently can be uncomfortable, particularly if you set yourself challenges and constantly strive to be better rather than settling for the *status quo*. However, the personal learning that can take place by exposing yourself to a range of different stimuli and understanding how to get yourself into a 'flow state' can be critically important.

Chapter 3 discusses in more depth the creative process, but it is really important to recognize that an individual's creativity will be stimulated by a number of influences, most of which are not found by sitting behind a desk in an office.

What are the implications of living outside the box?

There is a philosophical question: what box? Who has created the box? This operates at a number of levels, sometimes organizations create the big box. Managers create another box, teams, partners or our families another, and sometimes individuals create their own box until, like a set of Russian dolls, they find themselves feeling very small within the confines of life and work. To break out of this it is important to recognize the reality of the situation. It is about taking ownership. Some individuals may be very content inside their Russian dolls, it is a secure and comfortable place to be, and in a parental environment they become childlike. For some Mavericks this can bring out the worst of their behaviour – more destructive than constructive, to rebel rather than negotiate and ultimately to subvert. It takes a level of maturity to break out of this situation.

However, once this decision is made – if it is the right decision – individuals find a freedom of spirit that they had never experienced before. It does not work for everyone though, and it is important to test it first, to plan for it and as a number of our case studies suggest, try it out. If you never try you will never know and you could spend the rest of your life wondering 'what if'. Equally if it doesn't work out there may be other solutions: the patterns of employment in today's organizations are constantly changing, if you can embrace this change you may find a more elegant solution to the way that you can work with your organization.

If you do decide to work for yourself, there are many ways in which you can reduce the risk factor by identifying others who are like-minded, people who will be a valuable source of support and help you to build your own self-belief. However much we believe in our own ability, sometimes we need others to provide a sounding board, a link to normality to take us outside ourselves. What you don't need are intrinsically negative thinkers and unnecessary bureaucracy and this is one of the greatest challenges for organizations. Unfortunately too many talented people leave organizations because the battle for change is too long or complex.

Creativity should be celebrated, the joy of discovering something new, the euphoria of solving a problem, the craziness of a raw idea should be something that an organization cherishes, rather than holding it up for criticism. This is explored more in Chapter 3.

CHAPTER 3

'Fools, can't you see?'

Being different

This chapter is deliberately different; it tries to share some of the madness and fun of creativity that needs to be explored, and much of this is because creativity is about feeling. People who naturally enjoy exploring their creativity do see life through a different optic.

They often use their senses and operate through multiple intelligences. Creative people, when inspired, have an energy. It can also be a tiring experience, they may lock themselves away for hours working on an idea or a project. The title of this chapter was inspired by one of the respondents in the Maverick questionnaire who said that he had experienced so many moments when his ideas were way ahead of everyone else, and the only way he could sum it up was in the expression, 'Fools, can't you see?'

In the throes of creativity, people may be driven by a force which gives them an energy that others cannot quite comprehend. They have a passion to make something work, to find a new way of doing things, and often want to 'make a real difference' not just within their own working environment, but by doing something for the greater good of the organization or humanity in general. In pursuit of this they can become completely absorbed, and very frustrated when others do not have the same passions. This can be particularly true when waiting for a response or feedback from others. Because they invest so much personal energy and time in an embryonic idea, it can be very hard for them to then have to wait while their idea goes through a bureaucratic process before they get a decision about the acceptance of their idea. This often prompts creative individuals to leave an organization and to work for themselves.

One of the toughest parts of being driven by your creative thoughts is controlling this process and channelling it into a normal working environment. What is interesting is that if you have the inner flow of energy or ideas 'creation', you need very little to stimulate it. You may find that tools and techniques like Buzan's Mind Mapping® and de Bono's Six Thinking Hats help you focus. Mind Mapping® is a powerful way of expressing thoughts. The basic technique is to combine lines, text and images to represent related ideas and concepts. The technique can be used in a variety of contexts including note taking, summaries of visits, sales calls, problem solving, decision making, planning and designing training, life planning and career choices, etc. Buzan emphasizes the importance of seeing Mind Maps® as a whole-brain activity. One of the great advantages of Mind Maps® is that large amounts of information can be summarized on one page, and from the initial map project plans can be created. Further information is available through www.mind-map.com. With Six Thinking Hats, Edward de Bono shows how to maximize your own mind's effectiveness and help groups work creatively together. He uses a technique to separate thinking into different types. For further information contact www.edwdebono.com. These techniques can be helpful, however, if you have the ability to be creative all you really need is a means of recording, because when you find yourself in a creative state it is a force that cannot really be controlled, it has an energy and speed all of its own. Equally, it can disappear at will too. The good news is that it will return, often when you least expect it, nudging at the corners of your mind, saying 'Remember me?'

What do you do when you find that your mind is racing at 2.00 am, particularly if it is focusing on a non-work related subject that is close to your heart and you know that the next morning you are expected to attend an internal meeting which will sap all the remaining energy that you have? All you want to do is stay with the idea that demands your attention. This is a challenge faced by all creative people; there is also the need to respect and acknowledge the needs of others. In Chapter 4 the work of Bennis and Biederman in *Organizing Genius* is highlighted. In their study of Great Groups they describe how inspiring leaders strip out the non-essentials from the lives of their creative people, saying 'Great Groups are never places where memos are the primary form of communication'.

In the US in recent times the term 'duvet day' has been coined when people ring in and say that they are spending the day in bed recovering; they are not ill but simply exhausted. This has grown up in industries where long hours have become the norm and everyone recognizes that sometimes you just have to give in to the body's need to sleep. However, many traditionalists would criticize the concept and say that it is bound to be abused. Yet in naturally creative environments, where people are genuinely involved and excited by the ideas that they are developing, when and how they work is not the issue. In Ricardo Semler's *Maverick* he describes the working conditions within Semco, where there is huge loyalty that has been built up because individual needs are respected and individuals are given freedom. Semler says that he would rather create an environment where people *want* to come to work than one where they *have* to come to work and this is also borne out in the research by Bennis and Biederman.

Many working environments are far too serious and lacking in inspiration:

> 'When I get together with other musicians for a jam session, the group starts with a theme, plays with it, and passes it around. Suddenly the music lifts off, flies. We all fly with it ... It's an explosion of inspiration within art's given universe. No matter how high we fly we always return with something new, something we have never heard before. That's jamming. The management of creativity is rich in such paradoxes. It is both an art and a discipline... Jazz starts with a whim, a possibility, a "gut feel". If the whim continues to interest us we play with it. Our playing makes analogies and comparisons, entertains contradictions and variations. Development occurs. We get emotionally involved...
>
> 'All this is risky. Unavoidably so, when the alto sax player starts a solo he doesn't know where he is going, let alone how far and for how long. His inner voice – to which the music, other players, the setting, even the listeners contribute – direct him. That is the nature of improvization and companies that aren't willing to take its risks are not long for this fluid, protean constantly challenging world.'

> John Kao,
> *Jamming: The Art & Discipline of Business Creativity*

Creativity

Creativity is one of those words that prompts very different reactions from different people. For some, their eyes glaze over as if you are about to enter one of those 'soft areas' where they feel very uncomfortable. For others it prompts strong debate, 'you can't teach creativity, people either have it, or they don't'. Alternatively those who have experienced the power of being in 'flow' talk powerfully about how special the experience is. And then there is the reality…

To try and define the reality I have drawn reference from the writers mentioned in Chapter 1, my own research and feedback from those who took part in my study. As such it can only be another voice in the ongoing debate, because ultimately we all form our own view based on what we know and understand. The nature of creativity is such that we will always be discovering more. If we look back at some of the definitions in Chapter 1 pure creativity is very special, when it occurs it is perhaps best described as a 'state'. It reminds me of mercury, or quicksilver as it is sometimes described. Like mercury, when released creativity can permeate the corners of your mind, it can also be dangerous when released in an uncontrolled way. This analogy can be further applied to describing people when in a creative state as being mercurial, sprightly, sharp-minded and volatile.

You can use techniques to develop it and you can manage it, however it still retains its own unique powers, coming and going at will, seducing and enthralling those receptive to its magic. Merely describing it as a process is to deny some of its unique facets. If we were living in Ancient Rome, creativity would be found in a special bath where those fascinated by its waters would bathe, and having washed in its waters would be possessed with the ability to write, sculpt, paint or share the wisdom of their thoughts. If you filled a bottle with its water it would be priceless.

Why a bath? Water is often synonymous with creativity: immersing, letting thoughts wash over you, cleansing, limpid, calming, washing away grime or clutter, getting rid of stale thoughts; equally invigorating, powerful, energizing, or tranquil and relaxing after exercising your mind. It can also provide space away from others to think, even in today's society taking a bath, a shower or swimming are often solitary occupations. Walking in the rain may not always be pleasant when you're in a city or late for a meeting, but up on a hill or walking on a beach, rain may not just be pleasant but can clear the mind. Pictures of any form of water, from lakes, to the waves on a beach, to the silent ripples in a pool can provide stimulus to a mind willing to be stirred. Again the sounds and the feelings will stimulate the senses. This was particularly true in the responses in the Maverick study (see later in this chapter).

What could be equally likely is that in Ancient Rome those who bathed in the water and started to suggest doing things differently could have been thrown to the lions, because then as now being different would have had its price. Throughout history those who have created the most wondrous things were often only really recognized after their deaths.

> 'The trouble is that traditional organizations are not the most forgiving of environments. In many firms, failure carries the corporate equivalent of the death penalty. If you make a mistake, corporate Siberia beckons. This sends a signal to the corporate system that failure is punished. This not only stops people from failing – it stops them from trying. It leads to the building of systems that act against innovation rather than ones that nurture innovation. True innovators are prepared to fail in pursuit of unknown territory – *terra incognita* instead of *terra firma*... Traditionalists should remember the only way not to fail is not to try. And try we must.'

> Ridderstråle and Nordstrom, *Funky Business*

Allowing yourself space to think is critical. I once heard a phrase about needing to put a windscreen wiper over your mind to allow you to see through the accumulated clutter. Pure creativity often has to fight through so much rubbish and junk: accumulated facts that were given to us through our education that we have never used; day-to-day rubbish sent to us through junk mail, emails and memos; or even meetings that corporately we are meant to attend and yet through the window beckons a vial of inspiration essence if only we could reach out and pick it up.

In the late 1990s business writers were predicting that the vast majority of us would be working from home. There were predictions that we would have more leisure time, and yet today in corporate US, UK and Europe people are working longer hours than ever. Globally, technological advances mean that organizations rarely sleep, working virtually; while Europe is asleep the business runs through the Pacific rim, paying less for services provided by workers who are inducted into the culture of the country they are representing.

The irony of all this is that creative thinking is fast, it is frightening in terms of speed and complexity, because when your mind is flowing it is almost the equivalent of a mental meltdown. Techniques like Mind Mapping® help by allowing the thoughts to be captured on one page, along with the inter-connections. On a particularly good day the senses collide – hearing, seeing, feeling, sensing.

Mihaly Csikszentmihalyi, a University of Chicago psychologist, described this feeling as 'flow'. He says that we experience 'flow' when we feel in control of our actions and are masters of our own fate. What he discovered was that when people were experiencing 'flow' their state was very similar: there was a sensation of pleasure, they felt as if they were floating, they were totally immersed in what they were doing, they forgot their worries and lost sense of time. One of the challenges is to focus, because so many thoughts come floating into your mind it sometimes seems impossible to capture all the richness before the ideas dry up, or more likely before we are interrupted.

Many people feel that their best ideas occur when they least expect it, or when they're doing something else. However, once they start to flow you want to try to capture them. It is important to record everything, as even the most insignificant points may ultimately become an important feature of the end result. Equally, if you find that the ideas are not flowing it is important not to force the process, it is better to leave it and do something else. Often people find that by doing something completely different their mind will suddenly start generating ideas. Creative thinking also takes place at night through something called the 'Theta process', which is when the mind produces its own solutions, which are there when you awake. If you expose yourself to richness of experience you can stimulate your creativity by drawing from external stimuli and other pleasurable experiences.

In both these contexts it is actually very difficult to manage individual creativity. It is impossible to predict when individual creativity will start to flow, for many people it occurs out of work. Also, once it starts it is actually hard to stop. As a result, where an individual is expected to work within the constraints of a time frame, frustration, tiredness and ultimately lack of motivation often occur.

> 'The emotional foundation of the innovator at work is taking pleasure in originality. Creativity on the job revolves around applying new ideas to achieve results. People who have this knack can quickly identify key issues and simplify problems that seem overwhelmingly complex. Most important they can find original connections and patterns that others overlook. People who lack a flair for innovation, by contrast, typically miss the larger picture and get enmeshed in details, and so deal with problems only slowly, even tediously. Their fear of risk makes them shy away from novel ideas. And when they try to find solutions, they often fail to realize that what worked in the past is not always the answer for the future... People who are uncomfortable with risk become critics and naysayers. Defensive and cautious, they may constantly deride, or undermine innovative ideas.'

> Daniel Goleman, *Working with Emotional Intelligence*

As Goleman illustrates, one of the biggest frustrations for creative people is the justification that has to take place – not just through a bureaucratic process, but more often as a result of the fear or uncertainty of others. This often gives rise to the phrase that headlines this chapter, 'Fools, can't you see?' Ultimately what often happens is that people just walk away, because they get so despairing of the doubts and the questions levied by the risk-averse people.

It helps if you have a prosperous environment in which to experiment, but many Mavericks have started a business on a shoestring and a hunch. Unfortunately, at a time when an organization is wobbling, it is more likely to go tight than allow active experimentation. Words like retrenchment, cutting back and stick to the knitting (whatever that means) often sound the death knell to creativity. Also there is no perceived advantage in being different; witness the number of corporate organizations willing to pay vast sums of money to consultancies who come in and do exactly the same thing to you as they did to another organization and charge you the same amount of money as they charged your competitor to do the same thing. Re-engineering, competence frameworks, IT implementation, marketing, advertising, e-commerce, often follow a very similar model. In each case the client will be told of the need to come in and learn about you and it will take xxx weeks and cost xxx thousand of dollars. The good news is that at the end of the process we will make sure you have the same processes and competencies as your competitors.

> 'What was that?'
> 'You want to motivate your people and tap into their latent creativity?'
> 'Sure, that is in the competence model somewhere, but first let's concentrate on taking costs out, we'll get to people issues later.'

Far too many organizations normalize the ordinary and make scant attempts to accommodate or celebrate the extraordinary or different.

In the Maverick study there were a number of questions about creativity, the first one was:

'What are the best conditions that help you to be creative/innovative?'

The responses reveal a richness of stimuli, ranging across outside environments to organizational teams and an individual's own domestic space. As already indicated in this chapter, a number of respondents give examples of when they are in 'flow'. Freedom is often mentioned, as is feeling relaxed, and as mentioned in Chapter 4 when discussing preferred working environments, a need to be stimulated through their senses. Other people are also important for some respondents, either as a sounding board, or just having them around to talk to, socialize with, or to be there to welcome the individual back from their thinking time. Others mention that deadlines, challenges and pressure also help them to be creative. Quotes from the study appear in italics. Each new paragraph represents a new 'voice'.

I am most innovative when I am travelling in the car, walking in the countryside, in the bath, just before bed/first thing in the morning, usually those times when we sort of half switch-off. I am also very creative when I can bounce off others who are inspirational and innovative too. At those times the environment isn't that important because we sort of get caught up in the ideas and don't notice.

Quiet, thoughtful time, sometimes some calming or thought-provoking music.

Relaxing, drinking with friends.
Working with a team of friends to try to achieve difficult tasks.
The friend thing is important – a comfortable environment is important as is the feeling that my observations will be valued no matter how outlandish.

Freedom to explore new ideas, with others happy to contribute and add value. Requires trust and some basic processes to support.

Freedom to be responsible for myself. Supportive colleagues who are willing to experiment.
I need to know that everyone is 'busy' (eg during the workday or late at night).
I also need to move around and change the scenery a bit.
I need to take on my most complex thinking first thing in the morning.
It needs to be fun.
There needs to be someone else who cares about it.
I need social interaction.

I don't think there are best ones because I tend to be pretty good at creating them within most environments. I like to have people around to bounce ideas off. I like to have space and I like to be able to write large (flipchart, lining paper, BIG sheets or white boards).

Getting to know the people for whom the innovation is intended and their deeper beliefs, values and goals helps even more.

A stimulus – a challenge ('it won't work'); something new and 'interesting'; a deadline; others believe in my value.

Usually under pressure when the standard or obvious solutions won't work. I usually find that desperation is the mother of invention.

I like lots of quiet reflective time on my own, maybe with music and nature around, but I also know that I get sparks from contact with other people, from energy and noise, and from being forced to deliver within constraints. The key word is flexibility – the ability to move from one set of conditions to another as necessary or as the mood, context, people and process take me.

It obviously also depends on:

- *is this a solo piece of creativity or a team effort – what helps me be creative on my own (quiet, music etc) is not necessarily what will help to shift a stuck group*
- *the purpose – creative could mean high art or craft, or thinking about how to design a product*
- *is it something I have done before (leave me to it) or something brand new (let me reflect but give me information and prompts too)*
- *are we talking an exploratory step in the process, or a focusing step – different thinking styles and different conditions help.*

Creativity is not limited to 9–5. A variety of conditions, it could vary from being under pressure to after lunch, dozing, it's in that half-conscious connection with a near dream-like state that ideas can flow. Walking also helps.

Time away from my normal working environment is especially useful – at home, out and about visiting new places and seeing new things. These give me ideas and connections I would never have thought of back in my office, eg a north London temple tour I did recently with a friend, a day out with no intention of working, gave me loads of new ideas for reflection time intervals/activities in training events.

Usually at my best on a one-to-one with another who is receptive to and wants to co-create. Freewheeling, letting the thought processes take me.

Two very different ways – either alone and isolated from distractions (whether sitting daydreaming on a bus, walking across a field etc) or bouncing ideas with another person (or group) – the other person (or group) need not understand the problem/creative goal – they are there to act as coach/therapist.

In an environment that encourages creativity – no criticism for trying new things or having new ideas – opportunity to make mistakes or take risks without pressure of leadership getting mad – usually out of the office or away from the regular routine of each day.

Having a supportive 360 degree team. Having a boss that trusts me. Being with like-minded people. Not being forced to work in a regimented way. Working in a relaxed and non-bureaucratic/rigid atmosphere. Working in an informal environment but with a focus to keep me on track!

In a spirit of tolerance of difference and protective of ideas and of the self-esteem of others (there is a distinction here between being vigorous in testing ideas without being hurtful to the human source of the ideas).

Much 'politically correct' thinking is absolutely devastating for creativity. Self-esteem can be maintained without making people nervous/afraid to have fun, explore zany concepts etc.

When I'm with a group of others – often different people/disciplines. When listening to music or observing something closely. In my office – solitude, lights out, focused.

On a hillside overlooking the whole of Portsmouth, the Solent and the Isle of Wight, with a picnic, my bike and a glass or two of wine! So bottom line answer… where all my senses are being tickled but especially ambience, sound, visual etc.

Natural light, barefoot, somewhere relaxed. Bursts of no more than one hour.

Relaxation, freedom from stress and time pressure, support of colleagues. But after the creating phase I don't mind a deadline for the realization/report phase.

In a team situation, brainstorming with a good mix of theorists and practical people.

Sources of inspiration

The respondents in the survey had a whole range of sources of inspiration, again often focusing on the senses. Creativity is rarely something that encourages you to stand on the sidelines; people who are interested in discovering their creativity usually jump in with both feet, as these extracts illustrate.

Books, history, media, individuals who demonstrate abilities and the results I aspire to. I also believe I have inner sources of inspiration, call it will power, intuition, or spirit.

Time – My Self – Others – Inspirational People – Motivators – Those that live according to their own espoused values – Those that be rather than do.

Friends who are successful and creative. I have been privileged to work with two really creative individuals in my career; both were successful (in my view) iconoclasts. My own achievements at grammar school where I went from being bottom of the bottom class to top of the top class in three months. This taught me that almost anyone can do almost anything – provided they have the right support and motivation.

Music, clean architecture and environment, books, movies, travel.

For business creativity we use a lot of excursions, both linear and lateral to stimulate ideas. At home inspiration comes from being in nature, meditating, doing yoga and reading.

Film, internet, philosophy and young people.

Absolutely everything on the planet could be a source of inspiration OR a distraction.

Music; images (photographs/videos/graphic art); ideas; language (eg why do we use [this word] to mean [this idea]).

In no particular order: intuition, nature, children, people, Spirit (or God or whatever you call it/him/her), colours, life, situations, good design, good intentions, people expressing their true selves, stories, books, things produced with love, people caring about each other, travel, new experiences, old experiences, ideas, challenges, opportunities, tomorrow, next year, yesterday, childhood, death, sickness, health, passion, indifference, growth, restrictions, coincidence, plans...

Anything new, a place I haven't seen before, a picture on a card/post card, a quote I haven't heard before, lyrics in songs, videos, stories in books/ magazine articles, driving with nothing on my mind and suddenly a thought comes in that is somehow everything I have been waiting for but didn't know it.

I seem to find connections with things that others do not immediately see.

Life, experience, osmosis, colleagues.

God – family – wanting to be the best.

Events, other people, but mostly 'voices' in my head!

Thinking time and believing anything is possible.

Aesthetics, nature, music, people.

Environmental scanning, stimulating others, seeing is believing, therefore must travel, be out and about.

Writing, reading, serendipity.

Ideas and concepts and certain individuals from history. In no particular order I have been influenced in management by the writings of Bennis, Drucker, Blanchard, Peters and Handy. In history and philosophy by Gibbon, Toynbee, Hayek and Popper, among the Greats, Hobbes, Machiavelli, Burke, Mill, Socrates, Confucius, Lao Tse and historical Jesus. I also greatly admire Abraham Lincoln, Robert E Lee, U S Grant, Joshua

L Chamberlain, Churchill, Harry S Truman, Harold Macmillan and Margaret Thatcher.

The external, the senses, good people, fun people, the unusual, the young (oh, do I want to be young again, and have my time again), Garage music, Ibiza anthems, and before I die and assuming I am able I want to hire the Ministry of Sound!… and yes, I want to reach Maslow's self-actualization again!

What is the hardest part of being creative?

Respondents were also asked what was the hardest part of being creative; here are some of their responses:

Creative block probably.

Coming up with the initial ideas, also I find it difficult to 'create' around something that I personally have little or no interest in.

Nothing; creativity arrives out of the blue and is there or it isn't. I do not use tools like De Bono's etc to stimulate creativity. What I am good at though is using everything that I know, and putting different pieces together to make new patterns. It often works and saves loads of time. Nothing is really ever totally new!

Never believing that I am done or that it is good enough… Always seeing another path to go down.

Doing it to order.
Getting others to buy in.
Realizing that my idea is not necessarily the best.

Being misunderstood. In a commercial environment, the pressure to achieve can result in early parts of the creative process being regarded as 'strange'; unproductive; 'boffin-like'; learning from experience is 'talked' but not 'walked' enough.

Finding your true self underneath all the programming.
Delivering on the promise of the concept.

Being creative. Thinking up ideas is relatively easy, I suppose sorting the wheat from the chaff is the tricky bit and then implementing the end result.

Convincing others to see, believe and go for the opportunity that exists.

1. *Being creative on cue.*

2. *Recognizing the creative bit (you can overlook it).*

In convincing others about the utility of my ideas. Sometimes, I don't care.

I'm not sure I can answer this question, as I enjoy everything about being creative. Lying awake at night with ideas I treat as a gift, even if I'm not sure how I will use the ideas. I enjoy others calling me to pick my brains.

If I am honest, I guess the most frustrating feeling is that at some time others will get the idea too even though I had it first, eg recently someone suggested that a particular song was great to use on courses – I had been using it for eight months – so I guess I like to **be the first and the only***, once everyone is doing it I feel disappointed and want to find something else. Also I have a very vivid imagination – so staying in atmospheric hotels is very difficult – seriously, it has become almost impossible for me to sleep and this is definitely a bad thing.*

Finding employers and colleagues who really demand and can digest creative, non-conventional. Most people seek safety and familiarity.

Getting started with a blank sheet of paper on something outside of own experience.
Implementing it!

Knowing when to stop. An idea can be suffocated if focused on for too long at one time.

Employed: being constrained by bureaucracies.
Self-employed: lacking opportunities to engage in constructive discussion with peers.

Getting others to see what's inside your head and appreciate it.

Keeping in state.

Lacking resources – fighting for resources. Coping with conflict from change. Resistant colleagues, dismissive behaviour.

Being ahead of others and them not seeing the point.

Being prophet in my own land.

Explaining ideas to others.

Can't be creative on my own, but can formulate practical solutions from wacky ideas (usually not mine).

Maintaining the energy levels in the face of opposition.

The boring, boring old farts, people who lack enthusiasm and verve.
My strength… but some people wouldn't call it a strength… is that I have no problem in coming up with one, or five or ten ideas, and I don't care if all but one hits the deck as long as some ideas occasionally are used. I hate people who don't brainstorm properly. Just commit, commit and commit to paper, and then argue the detail on each later… but commit the ideas first.

What is the most rewarding part of being creative?

Creative people are sometimes accused of not having staying power; what is interesting is that many of the respondents cited seeing their ideas coming to fruition, or implementation, as one of the most important parts of being creative. A number of people mentioned the 'buzz', the energy, excitement and ultimately the pride of being involved in the creative process. For others it was important to be 'first' or different, and the disappointment when others caught up prompted them to want to discover something else that was new. Here are a selection of the responses:

Seeing your creations in use!

Seeing ideas coming into fruition and getting results. Solving problems and getting results using different approaches, getting people to think differently. I love the Eureka! moments when people's lights come on, I get a real buzz from this.

I guess the end result, the completed product or plan.

Seeing an elegant product/solution and having the appreciation of one's peers/colleagues.

The buzz of energy.

The buzz of achieving a breakthrough that makes others go 'great!' Then seeing it become real.

The fun of having an idea is good, but the real reward is when you see what you have created, whether it's in the garden or something you have published at work.

The people I get to work with.
Being able to create the world that I want to live in. Some of it isn't there yet but I'm working on it. It's all about the Henry Ford quote – 'Whether you think you can or think you can't you're absolutely right.'

The buzz of having a great idea.
The buzz of others recognizing this too.
The buzz of stimulating others.

Success. Knowing that you achieved something that was better and different from conventional paths.

The sensation when everything becomes clear and you have developed a concept (light bulb turns on).

Finding your true self and changing the programming.
Delivering on the promise of the concept.

Success, the fact that you, the team or the business succeeded in doing something that others didn't, couldn't or wouldn't see.

Sense of achievement and the resultant exhilaration.

Being different – if only for a while! Seeing connections before others.

Being praised for being creative is a motivation for me – as I was never good at drawing at school!! We now know that that doesn't mean that you are not creative but even now I would like to be able to draw and paint more than any other skill. So I guess getting some form of credit for being creative at all is a wonder to me.

Never running out of new product/service ideas.
Always being able to contribute something.

Originality.

Sense of personal satisfaction, when others get excited about a creative idea of mine.

Creation and connection with others and the moment.

To succeed.

The fun, and the difference, and the unusual, and the feeling of reward that you get… and indeed PRIDE.

Stages of creativity

Paul Torrance founded the creativity movement in education. He focuses on developing children's problem-solving abilities. This, he believes, supports the child's unique authenticity, his/her spirit. He defines creativity as:

Fluency: Thinking of many ideas

Flexibility: Thinking of different ways to do, or use things

Originality: Thinking of different unique things

Elaboration: Thinking of details and embellishments to an idea.

He states that it takes courage to be creative, 'Just as soon as you have an idea you are in a minority of one'.

Robinson and Stern, in their book *Corporate Creativity*, suggest there are four strategies that companies can use to promote diverse stimuli:

1. Identify stimuli and provide them to employees.

2. Rotate employees into every job that they are capable of doing.

3. Arrange for employees to interact with those outside the company who are likely to be the source of stimuli.

4. Create opportunities for employees to bring into the organization stimuli they get on their own.

A stimulus can either push someone in a completely new direction or give that person fresh insight into what he or she has already set out to do. What they also state is that what serves as a powerful stimulus for one person, for whatever reason, may not even be noticed by someone else. One of their most important findings was that rather than focusing on devising and delivering stimuli to a select few employees outside of their normal work, it is more important for a company to recognize that most stimuli that lead to creative acts will be found by the employees themselves; when they are, it is important that employees should have the opportunity to bring these stimuli into the organization and put them to use.

Supporting innovation

The generation of an innovation culture is seen as one of the most critical areas of focus for organizations in the 21st century.

Creative people are often viewed as being 'difficult' to manage, innovative organizations are perceived as being unusual, with a certain level of 'wackiness'. Tom Peters in his book *The Circle of Innovation* gives some fabulous examples of these viewpoints. He reproduces the following quotes from different writers:

> 'Our most beloved products were developed by hunch, guess-work, and fanaticism, by creators who were eccentric – or even stark raving mad.'

> Jack Mingo, author *How the Cadillac got its Fins*

> 'You say you don't want emotional, volatile, and unpredictable, just imaginative? Sorry, they only come in a package… I can offer you a dedicated, loyal, honest, realistic, knowledgeable package, but the imagination bit would be rather limited.'

> Patricia Pitcher, author *The Drama of Leadership*

All the best customer-focused organizations encourage individuals to take the initiative, to respond positively to challenge and to recognize the very real threat posed by competitors, and are driven to improve. Those who adopt a 'me too' philosophy will always be the ones who are in the slipstream of others.

Creating the 'right' environment, however, can be more of a challenge; lack of understanding about the process of innovation has traditionally led to people dividing themselves into two camps: those who are seen as creative and those who are not. This applies to an individual's assessment of themselves as well as the perception of others. By recognizing how the process of innovation works, individuals and teams can develop a clearer understanding and respect for each other's contribution. This is illustrated in the innovation process outlined in Chapter 6.

One model that you will see used in many contexts to describe the act of creativity is the one suggested by Joseph Wallas in 1926:

Preparation: Researching, data-gathering, primarily factual, you may have an idea of an area worth exploring, but it is unconfirmed, it may be nothing more than a 'hunch', or feeling.

Incubation: The ideas are beginning to form, but we let them simmer, we leave them at the back of our minds while we are doing other things, we bring them forward from time to time but we are not ready to act on them.

Illumination: This is the reason why a light bulb is often used to symbolize idea generation, or creativity. It is that stage or moment when you realize that you know what it all means or why you have spent so long thinking about something, it is often described as the 'aha' moment.

Verification: This is the checking out period, talking to others, sharing the idea, refining it, qualifying it, making sure that it really is worth investing time and resources in taking it forward into the next stage.

Other writers including Goleman have made reference to the work of Jules-Henri Poincaré and others in developing this model to include other stages, notably:

Execution: This is another important stage and it may sound the death knell for many ideas, as it takes a different set of behaviours and often requires the inventor to have to communicate and collaborate with others.

When you find that your creativity is being stifled, take a break and do something completely different. Take regular time out to indulge yourself, use others for support, and bounce ideas however crazy, build on initial fleeting thought to anchor more tangible concepts. Unlearn lessons from childhood: say 'I can' instead of 'I can't'. Tune into your surroundings by being inspired by a view, music, space. Some people find that they need to create a special environment to be creative, this may be a special place, a desk, or a room at home which becomes the focus for your thinking time. Other people go running, or take part in some other kind of physical activity. People who undertake a lot of travelling try to utilize this potentially 'dead' time to organize their thoughts.

Unlocking the windows of your mind...

As already mentioned, creative people enjoy thinking, are often used to spending time on their own so can be more introverted than others, and sometimes drift off into their thoughts for long periods of time. However, others find that they have less and less time for thinking. When did you last indulge in some thinking time? I don't mean the anxious trying to remember lists of information thinking time, but quality reflective thoughtful times, when you immersed yourself in thought so deeply that you almost had to physically drag your mind back to the present.

Throughout history there have been great philosophers who spent time deep in thought before they shared their ideas with others. In today's busy working environments, with or without open plan offices, people often find it difficult to sit quietly thinking without interruption. If you sat in a room without any visible signs of working you would inevitably raise comment.

Following a sequence, exploring options and allowing an incubation time are important parts of the creative process. Creative thinking time is a very precious commodity; allowing yourself time each day to explore ideas and new projects is critical to organizational and personal growth. Taking time out to think, co-ordinate ideas and chains of thought and re-order them into coherent actions is something that many of us rarely find time to do.

Yet not taking time to reflect, or to think before acting is one of the fundamental reasons why things go wrong in people's working and personal lives.

Why is thinking important?

Taking time to think allows you the opportunity of trying to make order out of chaos; unless you are particularly fortunate it is likely that your mind resembles a teenager's bedroom – clutter everywhere. Like the teenager you know that you have very useful information, but somehow you just can't find it when you need it. Equally you remember putting thoughts in a safe place, but they seem to get mislaid in the recesses of your mind. Each week you start with a resolute attitude of wanting to make a fresh start, but instead your mind becomes swamped again with emails, voice-mail messages, or people wanting to talk to you.

So how do you overcome this?

In reality it is similar to tidying a bedroom; the first thing to do is to recognize where you are starting from. What do you know about yourself? Have you spent time in the past analyzing your preferences about the way you like to work, your learning style, or have you undertaken any form of preference profiling or psychometric testing? Have you taken time to reflect on any of your learning or working experiences? It is important to invite feedback from others, but ultimately real learning takes place once you begin to understand yourself properly and to achieve this you need to understand as much about yourself as possible. It is also important to recognize what affects our thinking.

One very significant view is discussed by Daniel Goleman in his book *Working with Emotional Intelligence*. He reviews the work of a neurologist at the University of Iowa, Dr Antonio Damasio who, as a result of working with patients, had come to the following conclusion:

'Damasio's conclusion was that our minds are not designed as a computer, to give us a neat printout of the rational arguments for and against a decision in life based on the previous times we have faced a similar situation. Instead the mind does something far more elegant; it weighs the emotional bottom line from those previous experiences and delivers the answer to us in a hunch, a gut feeling... Just as there is a stream of thought there is a parallel stream of feeling... We have feelings about everything we do, think about, imagine, remember. Thought and feeling are inextricably woven together.'

Goleman uses the above comments as part of his description of our 'inner rudder' where he explores the role of intuition and gut feeling, and explains that such feelings shouldn't outweigh the facts but rather be included along with them. 'This sense of "rightness" or "wrongness" signals that what we are doing either does or does not fit our preferences, guiding values and life wisdom.'

What Goleman has raised in this book and in his initial book *Emotional Intelligence* is the importance of recognizing that while intellectual ability and technical expertize are important, it is our personal qualities, such as initiative, empathy, adaptability and persuasiveness that will guide us to success. Our thought processes are similar so that original thought may not come easily to us.

'Less than 15% of the people do any original thinking on any subject... the greatest torture in the world for most people is to think.'

The Great Quotations, edited by George Seldes

In order to take thinking seriously you need to prepare and create thinking time. It is also important to try and clear some of the unwanted debris that is cluttering up your mind. One important fact about the human brain is how much oxygen it needs to operate effectively: our brains amount to 2% of our body's weight but consume 25% of the body's oxygen intake, which is a very sobering thought when we consider most people's working environment. How often in a working day do you go outside to get fresh air?

As a starting point, try to create space to think, go somewhere quiet and just sit absolutely still, feel your heartbeat, become aware of sounds around you, feel the tension drain away. Initially you may find it hard to clear your mind, or to relax. For the first few times you do this you should be under no pressure at all to do anything, just sit still and enjoy the sensation of exploring your mind. Gradually you may find that you are able to begin to control your thoughts.

For example, if you want to trigger creative thoughts you can start to stimulate your mind by using a number of creative thinking techniques: word association, Tony Buzan's Mind Mapping® technique, or Edward de Bono's Six Thinking Hats. You can also order some of your thoughts through brainstorming, or using a more structured form of brainstorming by undertaking a SWOT (Strengths, Weaknesses, Opportunities, Threats) analysis.

One valuable use of thinking is to reflect on your achievements or your learning, eg:

Reviewing the past: What have I done, what have I learned as a result of my experiences?

The present: What do I need to think about? Why am I trying to find a solution?

The future: What do I really want to do? What do I want to achieve? Setting stretch goals, if I really wanted to challenge myself, how would I take my ambition further?

Use visualization to help you picture what it is you want to achieve, create a mental picture of what you want, really try and see the images, self-belief is a very powerful tool. When you find yourself in a situation that you are enjoying, practise using your mind like a camera, really absorb the images, the colours, try and capture the scents and sounds.

Try to recapture this later, your mind has the capacity to work for you, but it needs attention to achieve it.

When is it the right time to share thoughts with others?

One of the interesting things about focusing on your thinking is that you become more aware of what you can achieve; this is particularly true if you think positive thoughts.

What is important is that you share the right thoughts at the right time, because sometimes if we share our half-formed thoughts too soon, other people can be a negative influence on us and dampen our enthusiasm. However, we also often need a sounding board, someone we can trust with whom to share those embryonic ideas. As part of your support network, identify people who can give you balanced feedback, who will help you to explore your hopes, dreams and aspirations.

One of the really interesting areas is original thought, which is often harder to achieve. One of the reasons for this is that we often do not create the right environment for originality, or quite believe that we are capable of original thought. Like our intuition, or 'gut' reaction, original thought can be perceived as a bit 'scary', we may find ourselves with what we believe is an original thought and then be anxious because we have limited experience of being truly original.

This is the basis of true innovation, the 'aha' moment when you are faced with an opportunity that may bring competitive advantage, an advance in medical treatment, or just provide you with the opportunity to do something completely different with your life. Again this is the point at which you need your support network, people you can really trust to share your idea. Always be careful with your intellectual property, increasingly it has a value (see Chapter 8). If you take your thinking seriously, others will begin to develop respect for your knowledge.

If you are really serious about thinking, start by using the following checklist to help you prepare:

- What do I want to think about?

- When is the best time for me to think?

- What can I do to help my thinking?

- Who do I know that I can share my embryonic thoughts with?

- How can I create the right environment in which to think?

- Can I create a thinking zone, somewhere special where I can concentrate?

- Who do I know who will stimulate my mind and help me to think?

It is important to recognize how your thought process works and to remember to think about using your senses. The more you practise the more space you create for thinking and the richer will be the experience; you will come to cherish and value your thinking and reflecting time.

CHAPTER 4

Managing Mavericks

So how do you manage Mavericks?

In Chapter 7 we will be discussing how the way in which people are managed is often a contributory factor to absenteeism, why people suffer from stress, lose their temper or ultimately leave. For Mavericks the style of management is particularly important. How do you sit down with your manager and try to explain what you need when you may not really be sure yourself? Relationships can be particularly challenging for Mavericks: they do not particularly want to manage other people; neither do they want to be managed.

They do, however, want and appreciate support, but the timing of this is also important. After a period of intense creative thinking all a Maverick may want is just someone to unwind with; all the thinking, the puzzling, the working out of ideas is tiring, particularly if they have been shut away for some time. Having someone who will be a support- ive sounding board, someone almost just to 'hang out with' can be very valuable. The lives of Mavericks can often be a series of highs and lows, high activity followed by low energy, high volume of ideas – followed by nothing.

Living with this mercurial lifestyle can be exhausting both for the Mavericks and their colleagues/partners/families. 'Smoothing' their adrenaline can be almost impossible, it is not something that is particularly easy to turn on and off. Trying to accommodate this energy in a normal working or social environment can be difficult.

Bennis and Biederman in *Organizing Genius* make some very important points about talented individuals and organizations:

> 'In Great Groups the right person has the right job… Too many companies believe people are interchangeable. Truly gifted people never are. They have unique talents. Successful groups reflect the leader's profound, not necessarily conscious, understanding of what brilliant people want. They want stimulus, challenge and colleagues that they can admire. What they don't want are trivial duties and obligations; successful leaders strip the workplace of non-essentials.'

How would you define a Maverick?

This was a question asked in the study.

A Wild Card! Creative, slightly delinquent!

Someone who can see a way through a constraining mindset or set of bureaucratic constraints and consequently implements and/or drives a solution that results in achievement.

We all have an in-built compass that intuitively points us to our true purpose and vocation, it's that part of us that knows rather than thinks we know. Mavericks are people who use this compass to navigate life.

Someone who is prepared to be uncomfortable, and make others uncomfortable, to achieve against their aspirations, values and goals.

Someone who doesn't operate within the established rules.

A self-starter, someone with a clear understanding of what they want to do and who gets on and does it. Can't really be pinned down.

Subversive in the best possible way, innovative and driven to attain goals.
Not a team player.
The philosophy/ideology is more important than the job itself.
Will not quit.
Little respect for procedures and rules.

Someone who passionately lives life at both extremes, high and low.

A person who seeks adventure… only to find that, when she gets there, it becomes routine.

Someone who could just as easily be the life of the party or lonely in a crowd.

It's like climbing to the top of the tallest tree AND stepping out to the outermost branches. The view is fantastic, but the fall would be great. With no trunk to hold on to and nothing to break your fall, it is risky… physically and mentally.

Someone who is not afraid to do something radically different, to break the chains of expected behaviour or process, because they believe in themselves and the way in which they operate. Achieves results. Can sometimes be so single focused that they miss the views or support of others.

A person who a group would like to reject, but who hang on to them because they are so good at something and can't be replaced.

Someone with their own style; their own approach; but with real impact; gets a result for the business.

Its essence is best defined in the words 'some men see things as they are and say "why?" I dream of things that never were and say "why not?"'.

Someone who will do things differently just because they want to do things differently, not because different is what the situation needs.
Not necessarily creative – Mavericks can be destructive too.
Only a small percentage of the population.
Dangerous if they don't respect and value others – dictators and criminals are probably Mavericks.

Someone who takes calculated risks, sees opportunities, strives for success in the right way (living by morals and values), doesn't let problems or barriers stop them but rather looks at broader opportunities of how to get around the obstacle. Creates and inspires people they talk and walk with, not out of pure intelligence or aura etc but rather their conviction and passion for success and reaching success the right way.

Someone who realizes that the assumptions we make about the world are not set in stone but in sand. They only stand until the next tide of new thinking.

Genuinely unique in their thinking and the way they like to operate. Can not be managed like the followers, needs space and time to do their stuff. Not a prima donna, may be even quiet about their ideas – this is often when opportunities and ideas can get missed.

Breaking convention.

An outsider.

Someone who gets results but pushes the limits to do so.

Risk-taker; someone who doesn't recognize standard constraints; people energized by the dream rather than the process or simply the financial gain.

I see a Maverick as an employee who sees things differently and causes uneasiness among those engaged in groupthink.
Difficult to manage, internally motivated (ie often not requiring the motivation from a boss) but a potential source of sanity checking and creativity.

Someone who is barking mad, but whose ideas have a high degree of sense about them, when looked at carefully.

Someone who works to their own agenda for the greater good of their organization. Renegade, doing it differently, slightly off legality, concentrates on the outcome and not the process, out of the box, not frightened of being unusual or doing the unusual... but beware the Ides of March!... beware of the swords and the shoulder blades.

An individual who fails to conform to rules and procedure but actually outperforms his peers.

An individualist, with self-belief who paddles their own canoe and can be hard to manage.

One with a restless mind that knows there is always another way.

Someone like me! Not always easy to work with. Someone who does not accept easily tasks that seem pointless. Someone who needs freedom to make an occasional mistake in order to come up with the occasional big win.

Doesn't conform to the organization. Makes atypical career decisions/moves. Unpredictable but threatening only to how traditional thinkers might want the world to be like. Fun to work with.

Read Rosabeth Moss Kanter's booklet – 'The Story of O' *or* The Harvard Business Review's *article 'of Boxes and Bubbles'.*

A risk taker – someone who goes 'against convention' – they don't go with the flow.

Someone who does what they think is right irrespective of the norms and expectations of the organization or those around them.

Someone who follows their own lead and inspires others.

If you are fortunate enough to get close to a Maverick, just take time to observe what it is they are really offering you, or the organization. Think back over your life and recognize those who have created something special – it may be an artistic creation, or the application of an idea. Some people may be described as a genius, but as Bennis and Biederman have showed in *Organizing Genius*, it is the application of their ideas through active collaboration that really brings results. Anyone can have a great idea, but having the passion, drive and commitment to implement it is something that sets people apart.

What is it really like being a Maverick?

In many ways being a Maverick manifests itself as a difference. A feeling that wherever you are there will be periods of time when you need to withdraw, to be on your own, to take time to think. In terms of inter-actions with others you may be like a chameleon, very few people may actually see the real you. Used to being different, individuals (particu-larly in corporate life) learn to handle the difference and 'smooth' some of their behaviours to conform to an organizational norm. One of the most frustrating aspects is the time-wasting, the stifling of creativity and the slowness of decision making.

Mavericks struggle to manage their boredom, stimulated and energized by new ideas they often find the process of moving from the dream to reality tedious. Exponents of the 'Just do it' school of thought, they find it incredibly difficult coping with the lack of speed in implementation. Raising finance for a project or going through due diligence processes is often a challenge, as James Dyson describes in Chapter 8. Normally preferring activity to inactivity, sitting in meetings reading lengthy documents can be painful for them. However, creative problem solving, lateral thinking, even following a logical process can be easily absorbed into their quick-thinking minds.

What really delights a Maverick is finding like-minded people with whom they can bounce ideas, who convince them that they are not alone in their thoughts. This will impact enormously on their relationship with an organization. If they find themselves in a team of like-minded people their output can be tremendous, because shared thinking in a supportive environment can be a very positive experience. If they are part of a team where they are the only one perceived as the 'ideas' person it can be more of an isolating experience, particularly if the rest of the team think very differently and they have to spend lengthy periods of time convincing others of the need to do things differently and justifying their ideas.

As well as sponsoring innovation, organizations need to recognize the importance of realistic test-beds, where ideas can be experimented with, realistic, objective feedback can be sought and the idea can be vigorously tested. It is a fine balance between active experimentation in a safe environment and indulgence. Individuals, teams and organizations need both to sponsor innovation or creativity and to set it into a pragmatic reality – when the balance is right great progress can be made.

Equally important is the recognition of the need to have a process that supports innovation as well as people who can generate ideas. Creative people, Mavericks, entrepreneurs, often get bored easily, because of the speed at which they think: because they do spend time thinking things through, it is very frustrating to then sit through lengthy meetings waiting for either internal gatekeepers, or external investors to reach the same conclusion.

The ability to assimilate knowledge and concepts means that it is easy to get enthusiastic about a lot of ideas, projects, new business opportunities and then to become over-committed. If you can see solutions to problems you may not see risk in the same way as others. Many people in the case studies in Chapter 9 and the people who responded to the Maverick questionnaire feel that they have a social responsibility. They often care passionately about people and their individual freedom to develop their potential. They are perplexed by the way organizations make it so difficult to make things happen and to achieve organizational change. They often have a logical common sense approach to life and readily find solutions. They simply don't see the barriers erected by others who are more cautious.

However, those who have experience of years of working in corporate environments have learned to modify their behaviour and to be more cautious, even though intuitively they believe they know the right way to do something they will still check it out logically. Sometimes they acknowledge that they have perhaps been over enthusiastic, but they handle risk with a positive attitude. Interestingly, as they move towards the end of their careers they often find the assurance and courage to become more of their own person. Disenchanted with corporate life they may go out and run their own business. They may decide to create a business, or work for themselves, but whichever route they choose they usually want to allow themselves more of what they wish they had been given earlier in their careers.

One of the interesting facts is that creativity, innovation and Mavericks are not always linked. Creative people are not necessarily innovative, Mavericks are not necessarily creative, and Mavericks are not always innovative. What can be a most potent mixture are creative Mavericks who want to innovate. Discovering them and helping them to channel their talent is like finding liquid gold.

What is important is that they want to work with an organization. There has to be a desire, people cannot be ordered to be creative and a number of the participants in the questionnaire have made a choice not to be employed by an organization.

'Managers cannot demand creativity any more than they can order growth from a flower.'

John Kao, *Jamming: The Art & Discipline of Business Creativity*

What do Mavericks want?

One of the areas covered in the Maverick study was how much responsibility the participants wanted; three questions were asked:

How much responsibility do you want?

- *managing yourself*
- *managing others*
- *managing process.*

In the sample there was an overwhelming response to 'managing yourself'. Almost all respondents wanted responsibility for managing themselves to a greater degree, varying from 50–100%, but with the majority wanting the responsibility. Some made additional comments such as:

Much as practicable, but I admit that I love to have peer support.

Definitely I don't respond well to being overseen.

Absolute – very independent, would rather not have anyone telling me what to do.

High, I want to feel in control of myself.

I need a lot of freedom, but staging posts/deadlines are essential.

Full responsibility, but sometimes, purely as a change it is nice to receive direction and be absolved of responsibility, not for long though.

When questioned about managing others there were some fascinating responses. The majority did not want responsibility for 'managing' others, however a number made the distinction between managing and coaching, or guiding:

Delegation is very important. Once the concept is fully formed I want to inspire others to help bring it to fruition.

Yes, quite enjoy coaching people in my team and bringing them on.

There was also a preference for working with self-motivated people:

Guide not controller – only like working with self-motivated people.

Depends – if it is co-ordinating other self-motivated people that's OK; not if it's telling people what to do.

There was also a desire for other people to take responsibility for themselves:

Yes, for those that don't need to have their hand held.

It's a necessary part of my job but I would prefer that my team took a high level of responsibility for themselves (and am encouraging them to do so).

Some respondents also saw it as a more long-term opportunity, others made the link between the way that they were managed and the way they wanted to manage others:

I liked managing others because of the clear development of people's talents, confidence and skills in the environment I encouraged (eg two current directors of large companies started with me as junior staff).

A high degree of autonomy, as a director once mentioned to me, his job was often to aim the rifle, my job was to be the bullet which was fired out and rapidly hit the target. He wouldn't or shouldn't have to make major alterations rather through coaching, discussions and advice slightly nudge the direction of the bullet (ie me). I see myself performing this type of role for people who report to me.

I don't mind being managed if my workstream and ownership of that workstream are clear. Managing others is key to testing and refining your own creative ideas and style, but I need adequate time to coach and manage others. I get frustrated just handing out orders. A creative person also requires quality alone time, not persistent team interaction.

For many it was not something that they really wanted to do, either because they had no real interest in it, or as a number of respondents said that as they got older they wanted to do it less:

I've done this and been good at it but I really like not doing so.

Have previously managed a small team of people, my personal difficulty comes with confrontation, I like to work with consensus as opposed to an 'Iron Hand'.

As much as it takes to get the job done – responsibility comes from what I do, not from what I am granted or given.

After 25 years of doing it, I'd rather not be bothered any more! I like working with self-motivated, self-starters who I can trust to get on with it. I no longer have any patience for all the little mundane personnel hassles that are involved in organizations.

The responses to how much responsibility for managing process people wanted varied enormously; some people, as in their responses to managing others, gave an emphatic 'none', while others were interested but not as a main preference. What was apparent was that a number of respondents recognized its importance. Some wanted a consultative way of doing it:

Like a process that brings everybody into a common purpose. Dislike management systems, which have everybody working in different directions or on own pet projects.

I think the managing process should be consultative yet decisive. Focus on results and success. Deal with problems constructively and promote the notion it's better to have tried than not having tried at all.

Others recognized its importance, but wanted less to do with it directly:

Less interesting for me – like to come in once needs have been identified, do my stuff and let the organization follow through. I know if it has worked well from my perspective, being a lone ranger I cannot and do not expect to be solely responsible for the complete process... I'm bigger picture motivated and a doer, less interested in booking venue, photocopying etc.

No thanks! But seriously, it is necessary in business to have some process and it can assist Mavericks to get their ideas progressed and adopted if it has been through an agreed process.

Without doubt some people had strong views about an approach to 'managing process':

Managing is a process in itself so how do you process a process?
I believe there is a lot of wrong thinking at a fundamental level about 'what', 'is' and 'how'. There is a case for applying basic philosophy and epistemology (of which NLP – Neuro Linguistic Programming – is only one) to the particular context one is considering.

People are sometimes too busy 'processing' (whatever it is – head down, to notice the reality of a particular situation). They tend, for example, to confuse process and outcome. But what do I know?... this ain't mainstream – this is maverick stuff!

Everything's a process and processes are much misunderstood and maligned. Don't get me on this topic or I'll ramble on all day.

As well as asking individuals about how they liked to manage there was also a question about what management style they would prefer and there was an unquestionably united response to this:

*Enabling and empowering. 'Go do it and **** up if you need to' was one of the best pieces of advice I ever got.*

Motivational – Herding – Charismatic – Exploratory – Time for Everyone – Confident – Visionary.

A true coach… one who allows a round table and good feedback with support.

I really hate being managed so the best management style is one that agrees what's needed and then trusts me to deliver.

Trusting and hands off where talent is valued, with positive tolerance of diversity and ambiguity.

Others emphasized the importance of a balanced approach, wanting some direction or guidance and then to be left alone, but still to feel that their manager was interested and able to offer support if needed:

Hands-off; available; support AND challenge (in that order).

Very clear objectives, balance risk and prudential judgement.

Agree a desired outcome, contract the terms and conditions and leave me to it, but stay interested.

Challenging, decisive, calculated risk taker, team orientated, values input, not control orientated.

Definitely empowering, often criticized in the past for not being involved enough (not by my staff I hasten to add, but by those above me!). Trust that the people I have recruited can do the job and will call if they need me. Then I can be a coach or instructor depending on the needs of the individual.

Trusting, supportive and unobtrusive.

Hands off, but definitely there…

Based on trust.

Both focused and loose.

Treated as equal.

Some also emphasized the importance of working in teams, citing self-managed teams as a preference:

Definitely team… I really believe in forming, norming, storming, performing and also like Belbin.

Un-bureaucratic and non-hierarchical. Flexible teams are important.

Leaders that model the behaviour they expect from their teams – leaders that are committed to growing other people.

One respondent gave a similar comment to the one suggested by Peter Honey (see Case Study, Chapter 9):

'Ask for forgiveness, not permission'.

In an ideal world how do you like to work?

As well as management style there were five other areas about ways of working covered in the Maverick study.

Environment

For many of the respondents, playing to their senses is important: people also emphasized their desire to vary their surroundings; and while individuals often prefer to work alone, many also need access to other supportive colleagues. What is also interesting, is how many times people mention the outdoors, which is a testament to the need to give people freedom from the confines of the office:

Good Light – Fun People – Funky Stuff – Strong Music – Open Spaces – Water – Trees.

Spacious, light, minimal furniture, quiet.

Calm, quiet, uninterrupted.

On the beach.
With access to friends in order to chat informally – about anything – just to free my brain up; relaxation and the ability to talk loosely around issues is very, very helpful.
Lunch, tea breaks with friends are very important for stimulating discussion.

Informal, relaxed, with others (I am an extrovert).

Mixture of quiet and solitude for crafting/writing and stimulating meetings with others to get ideas and team spirit.

Sun, fresh air (no air conditioning please), water nearby!

Comfortable, casual, bright, fun… with sound in the background.

Plenty of stimulation, books, music, but also with space for quiet reflection, walks in the woods etc.

Open – literally and metaphorically; with people who ooze fun and optimism.

Mix of everything – sometimes quiet, sometimes loud, sometimes at home, sometimes not, sometimes in country houses, sometimes in cities.

Airy, plenty of light. Having an open dress code.

Wherever felt comfortable that day – the office, home, garden, café, driving around.

Good ergonomics. Good quality IT infrastructure and communications. A nice view is helpful. Working from home is good but I need the opportunity to mix with colleagues often.

Where the senses are being tickled… eg a view, nice furniture, a bar, Dartmoor, a darkened room with candle and or loud music to my taste.

Work colleagues

This is one of the really fascinating areas about how Mavericks like to work and in many ways reflects the different stages of the creative process. When describing how they prefer to learn (see Chapter 5) a number of the respondents said that they like to learn through reading and others need periods of time to reflect; both activities are often carried out in a solitary state. Others, however, expressed a need to meet with friends or colleagues for brainstorming, idea bouncing sessions. Reacting specifically to a question about work colleagues their responses were as follows:

Like-minded, inspiring, interesting, positive, forward thinking, sense of humour, creative, supportive, partnership.

With similar people – creative, open to change, 'doers'.

Yes, with bright sparky people.

Open minded people with strong values.

Who I choose – they tend to be people I resonate with but then I resonate with lots of different types of people.

A good mix of 'types' but where ideas are as important as the 'product'; optimists.

Eccentric and individual. Able to work within a team without losing their personal identity. Creative but pragmatic.

Positive and empowering people please.

Yes, with a range of skills that complement mine, a good sense of humour and flexible attitude. Having the opportunity to engage in banter and discussion is very important to my creativity.

Diverse, willing to learn, able to admit mistakes... and learn.

In creative group or with one other.

Sometimes I prefer to work on my own.

Mostly on my own but enjoy regular revitalization with a particular group of friends/associates once every three months at a network meeting.

For gossip only.

Yes, but to bounce off… but they have to be sympatico and do it in way that suits me… and have fun doing it too.

Hours

One of the real issues for Mavericks is when they want to work because both the individuals interviewed in the case studies and those who responded to the questionnaire find that they get their best ideas and feel at their most creative: either when taking part in an activity, like walking, running, or swimming, or at strange times, such as early in the morning or late at night. This is evidenced by their responses to the question about the hours that they preferred to work:

Short periods of time interspersed with time out – eg day on day off, week on, week off, work for a month take a month off.

Early morning – late evening.

Hours: 11am – 7pm

When I feel like it; sometimes though when working alone the very early or very late parts of the day are when ideas slip into place. Going for a run also helps relaxation and enables my subconscious to unravel problems. When I finish running I often get a really good answer to the problem that has been bugging me; alternatively I realize that the problem is either avoidable or indeed part of the solution!

Any time (I mean flexible) (a number of the respondents gave this answer).

Flexible as opposed to always long!

Flexible, with a 'deadline' insofar as I need to focus on finishing.

When I choose (a number of the respondents gave this answer).

Any and all hours, ideas know no bounds.

Unstructured/'permissive'/self-imposed.

Whenever need/are inspired to work.

When it fits with the task and with life, so that varies daily. Some focus is necessary though to limit rambling!

Flexible, work to exceed outcomes, by this I mean sometimes longer hours sometimes shorter (40 hrs to 60 hrs depending on how energized).

6.00am – 3.00pm

6–7 hours per day, after lunch until evening.

Late start, late finish (10 – 7.00) at best three-quarters through day.

Equally an increasing number of people are making lifestyle choices and consequently build some of their creative time around their family:

After 9.30 (I enjoy dropping the kids off to school and the walk often throws thoughts into my mind that I will have to do something with when I get to the office) and until I feel spent! Sometimes 3.00pm as I can work through non-stop without even stopping for a coffee. Other times starting later. Often in hotel rooms away from home I get the chance to think 'out of my usual box' and can write/sketch well into the night.

Flexible, but I'm most creative in evening hours.

What's needed to get the job done while ensuring my family are my top priority.

If work is fun, hours tend not to be an issue – I have often sent people home!

Best early in the day. Often ten hours.

2000–0200.

There were also direct contrasts between responses such as 24/7!! and 9am – 5.30pm, Mon – Fri.

Employed v self-employed

The question that probably causes most challenges for Mavericks was whether they want to be employed, or self-employed and some of the most poignant statements came in this part of the questionnaire:

Employed for mortgage comfort… but with this comes huge frustrations about having to answer to others, and they add extra burden, eg they do something so so differently from how I would do it. In my dreams I would like to be self-employed… But haven't got the guts… but I know it's the right way.

Employed? Yes – like the safety factor.
Self-employed? If necessary but I can't sell.

Employed? – Only if the management style suited me.
Self-employed? – Yes.

Employed? – Not again!
Self-employed? – Yes.

Self-employed?
Prefer self-employed because so few organizations create, or even seek to create such an environment in the UK. USA much better in this respect.

Employed? Work best in a small team of like-minded people.
Self-employed? Not best at working on my own.

Employed – Less hassle than self-employment but normally imposes considerable constraints both on freedom to act and also flexibility to work. Self-employed? Fine, but subject always to the problem of both delivering contracts and finding new ones. Can be lonely.

Employed? Unlikely.
Self-employed? Or contract basis preferred. For me my autonomy is important.

Employed? In a small group that feels like family/friends... with variable roles.
Self-employed? Doubtful, as I am buoyed by the team, and I get lonely easily.

Employed? – small business unit within a larger organization = small, yet cushioned from hard knocks.

Employed? Yes, more than likely, while I feel I would like to be self-employed, the security of employed status still provides some 'apron strings'.

Employed? Rarely.
Self-employed? Even when employed.

What do Mavericks want from an organization?

This was another question in the study: What do you think Mavericks want from an organization? In reality, Mavericks want much the same as any other employee, they just may be able to articulate it more strongly. They do, however, also suggest some additional things that organizations may find it harder to provide:

Freedom, no blame, risk taking.

The opportunity and the freedom to innovate and create, lead others and impact business results.

Recognition, freedom of expression; an opportunity to shape the destiny of the organization.

Recognition that they can contribute in a positive sense, and not always be seen as a problem. Allow them to play to their strengths.

To change it by disruption! Otherwise they should leave and succeed in a more appropriate environment.

Personal acclaim and recognition through their achievements and results.

In my case, very little interference and lots of support. Mind you, the danger with this question is that it assumes that all Mavericks are alike. Pretty much by definition they must not be so the question itself is risky.

Resource to pursue their dreams.
Recognition of their genius.

The chance to excel and to be better for it.

Praise, power.

Not to be in it.
Money.
Personal recognition – which is what the non-mavericks want too but are less willing to show it or they get it in other ways (eg some people get personal recognition by being told they fit in).

Opportunities to make their difference useful.

Flexibility, guidance, understanding of some form of parameters, a safe belonging.

Recognition of this skill called 'creating' and of having that skill.

A machinery to implement their ideas. Mavericks by definition are non-conformist; perhaps hate orderliness. Implementation of the idea – innovation – requires highly organized effort, which by definition is not what the mavericks enjoy doing. Hence, they look for a support mechanism. Organizations which can provide this will excel in the marketplace.

To be listened to, to be given the space and time they need to think things through and investment to try things out.

Flexible role and work schedule.
Absolute meritocracy, not treading the same promotional path as everyone who goes before.

To be recognized for their ideas and energy and not vilified for speaking their minds. To be understood and 'tolerated' by the organization. To be allowed to challenge the boundaries (what boundaries?).

The ability to use its resources to meet their own ends – this sounds parasitic but it isn't. The organization gains a lot from the maverick constantly pushing at the boundaries of what is/isn't the norm in the organization.

They probably don't want organizations at all – but see them as a means of achieving personal ambitions. Therefore when involved with organizations they seek space, recognition, opportunity and advancement.

Space to build the dream. He/she needs to be unfettered and not have to account for process.

Appreciation of their contribution and tolerance.

Nurturing and adulation.

The environment that they need to optimize their creativity and innovation… whatever that is for them… and each Maverick will have different needs.

A channel for creativity, support and freedom to exercise ideas. Challenge to make things happen.

Acceptance that it is okay to be a Maverick, that organizations need Mavericks, not too many, but a few.

Challenge at one level, but compliance at another. They often fight organizations or are evasive.

Recognition, someone to continue the process, peace.

They need 'back office' help, admin support.

To subvert it from within. Working for an organization which was not so desperately in need of change would actually be rather dull.

Recognition of worth, opportunity to operate.

How organizations frustrate Mavericks

If we review the responses from the questionnaires and the case study interviews there are a number of ways in which organizations frustrate Mavericks. What is so striking, however, is that so many of the frustrations could be eradicated comparatively easily if there was better communication, respect and understanding of individuals. It is not just an issue for Mavericks, many people are frustrated by their organizations. Some of the key issues for Mavericks are when people don't believe in them, or their ideas. Equally, although it is important to look for balanced feedback, sometimes for a Maverick it can seem that the feedback is more negative than positive. This can be particularly so in the more innovative ideas or process improvements.

Sometimes Mavericks reach high levels within an organization. A Maverick on a corporate board can split a boardroom if not handled properly; equally an entrepreneurial CEO with Maverick characteristics can struggle to grow an organization unless he can develop an infrastructure, which can support him during this period.

Mavericks often see things differently. They have no problem with thinking outside the box; their difficulty is more likely to be in focusing on the everyday and more mundane activities. They can cause problems in some organizations by wanting to disturb the *status quo*, and in not wishing to see things through to the end, ie they may passionately argue for something to be done differently, and then lose interest as soon as they get permission to change.

To work with a Maverick you need first to understand them and their unconventionality. They are easily bored and are constantly in need of new challenges. They may have a strong value system and are unlikely to be swayed away from an intuitive decision. They believe passionately in particular causes and their emotions may be close to the surface.

When do organizations need Mavericks?

If we substitute the word Maverick for people with vision, entrepreneurial spirit, creativity and commitment to doing it differently it may be easier to answer the question. Many entrepreneurs could be described as Mavericks, and at the start of a business they have the very qualities that are needed; however, as the business grows they often need support to help them maximize the potential of their business. If we refer to the Innovation 3® six-stage model of innovation described in Chapter 1 (creating the climate; idea generation; developing and exploring ideas; evaluating options and decision making; making it happen, implementing innovation and measuring success, monitoring innovation) it is easy to recognize and understand why this happens. At the start of a new business it is important to have clear vision and the energy to handle the initial stages of a 'start-up'.

These embryonic businesses are often staffed by sole traders, partners or a small team. At this early stage energy and enthusiasm will go a long way towards business success, but this will not necessarily sustain the business in the long term. What will be needed are individuals who can operate at each stage of the growth of the organization. One of the major issues for SMEs (small and medium-sized enterprises) is the ability to grow while still adhering to the vision and values of the original owner.

Large organizations and Mavericks

As identified above many Mavericks are self-employed, freelancers or sole traders. The reason for this is often that they leave the larger more traditional organizations because they become frustrated trying to fit in. However if an organization can understand and recognize how creative people operate they will be better able to create an environment that fosters and encourages Mavericks to stay. This is discussed in more detail in Chapter 7.

What can a Maverick offer an organization?

Interestingly, organizations are beginning to recognize the importance of retaining people who think differently. There are beginning to be reports of 'creative' thinking individuals who are employed for their 'ideas'. In some cases there are quite unusual arrangements where an individual is employed purely to think 'outside the box'. You will hear comments about how an individual comes into an organization, shares ideas and leaves again. However, in the sharing of 90 ideas (only one of which might be worthwhile) Mavericks can challenge the *status quo* of an organization; they suggest creative ideas and ways of doing it differently. Sometimes it can be as simple as asking the question 'Why, or why don't we?' Some organizations such as 3M and Disney are known for the opportunities they provide for individuals to be creative, but why are there comparatively few such companies?

A Maverick can bring an injection of energy, creativity, a spark of enthusiasm which can energize an organization. Nurturing it however can be difficult, organizations often experiment with the concept of 'think-tanks' or fast track high potential. In reality the whole organization needs to embrace innovation and creativity, create environments where idea generation is respected, where it is okay to fail (provided the lessons learned through the failure are built on in the future) and where people who think differently are respected for their views rather than ridiculed. For most organizations this represents a fundamental shift in the way they recruit, induct and retain staff. If we refer to the model below, this is a dynamic way of switching the organizational focus from the past to the future.

As we move further into the 21st century the need to continuously innovate will not go away, the need to retain talent and to manage the Mavericks will continue to be critical. As Goleman describes:

> 'The premium on emotional intelligence can only rise as organizations become increasingly dependent on the talents and creativity of workers who are independent agents... Such free agents suggest a future for work somewhat akin to the functioning of the immune system, where roaming cells spot a pressing need, spontaneously collect into a tightly knit, highly co-ordinated working group to meet that need and dissipate into a free agency as the job finishes. In an organizational context such groups may arise within and across organizational boundaries as demands require, then cease to exist once their task is accomplished... Such virtual teams can be especially agile because they are headed by whoever has the requisite skills rather than someone who happens to have the title "manager".'

World view – desire to make a significant contribution
Really make a difference, capacity to blue sky, to think outside the box
Ability to reap and garner experience – corporate ability to flex, adapt and learn from the past
Individual capacity to coach, develop others and cope with ambiguity – openness to experience
Desire to recruit, retain and develop talent
Ability to germinate and grow new fruits, seeds and future corn

© The Inspiration Network

So what do you do if you think you are a Maverick?

This was a question that I asked all the case study participants and their responses are in Chapter 9. However to summarize the key points, one of the first things to recognize is that whatever anyone else says you have to identify for yourself whether you are a Maverick, or someone who thinks differently. We all have choices in life; some of the respondents in the questionnaire show that these choices are never easy. Declaring your difference has associated risks, whether you are eight or eighty.

Most people and organizations like conformity, they are suspicious of non-conformity, which can appear threatening even if it is marginally different from the norm, eg a child who answers questions from a teacher with enthusiasm. A child who constantly asks 'Why?' A young adult who declares that they are not going to university, but wants to run their own business instead. A woman who wants to combine having children with a career and a social life too. A man who wants to spend less time working and more time with his children. Elderly people who want to carry on working. Pensioners who want to do all the travelling that they could not afford to do when they were younger. Workers who want to make suggestions to the executive board about what the customers really want. Lone individuals who create something so unique and special they are scared of sharing it. Each are different in their own way and each may receive challenges or criticism from others, but ultimately it is about personal choice.

Every individual is unique and will have different learning styles, different ways of managing, coaching and developing people and preferences in the way they work or interact in a team. There are however some common characteristics about people who are creative, innovative and display Maverick behaviour and these themes come through in both the case studies and in the responses to the questionnaire. These people are committed to exploring, to discovery, they are often driven by an inner energy. Some are very competitive, and like Ian Banyard (see Case Study, Chapter 9) could be described as a 'polarity responder', while others want to make a real difference in the world.

Every individual has the right to give themselves permission to be different; but there is also the need to recognize what this may mean. People who are driven by their own personal energy and creativity, people who passionately believe that they want to do things differently also need to be able to create an environment that can support this difference. A number of the case study participants talk about what they have done, or continue to do to sustain themselves: through personal development, therapy, finding close support from others, developing a group of like-minded thinkers, reading, questioning, thinking, reflecting, working on unusual projects, travelling, using their senses and discovering each day something new about themselves or others.

They also recognize the fallow time, the times when they don't succeed, when their ideas get rejected and when they get frustrated with their own projects. When the adrenaline that normally drives them fails, when they get ill, when their bodies cannot keep up with their mind. All the case study participants can cite examples of times when it didn't work for them, when they got burnt in a situation perhaps by taking a risk that didn't work out, when they pursued something even though their intuition told them not to. Hard though those times are, they equally know that if you have the ability to be creative, it will flow again. Sometimes we just need to turn the engine off before starting over; people who are creative often find that their internal engine is running at higher revs than others and like a car you may well need a service, a changing of plugs and a complete change of oil – without this you can keep going but your engine may just get more and more sluggish. Sometimes we just need to stop, have a full 'health check', valet and polish!!

CHAPTER 5

Maximizing high potential

Retaining talent

As discussed in chapters 3 and 4, retaining talent is not just about Mavericks, it is also about the recognition that all individuals have a contribution to make, not just for the benefit of the company, but also for their own personal development.

Talent is quite an emotive word and we each have our own interpretation of what it means. It is not solely about retaining creative people, but it is often the people that think differently who become frustrated and leave; there are only so many times that you can take rejection of the ideas that are important to you.

Being different brings its own set of frustrations; so many people who show originality and personal drive are viewed with suspicion by others. It often starts early: naturally enthusiastic children soon learn through peer pressure not to respond to the questions posed by their teacher; enthusiasm drains to acceptance of the reality that others may not understand and may ridicule or challenge what you know to be true. Usually the biggest frustration occurs when a creative person reaches a conclusion and then has to justify it, or explain it to others; often they do not remember how they got there, they are just convinced that it is right.

There are two sides to this: often they are right, but sometimes there are spectacular failures fuelled by someone playing a hunch. Again, it may not be that it was the hunch that was wrong, it may be the circumstances that occurred in and around the inception of the idea that were not right. One of the biggest issues for individuals is how long organizations take to give feedback on ideas submitted; this has particular relevance for Mavericks.

Imagine that you have been thinking about the idea for some time, it has gone through all the stages of incubation and you excitedly emerge with the 'Eureka' moment to come face-to-face with others completely unaware of the process you have undergone; what then happens is often rejection. Sometimes with a flat refusal, with no explanation, or a series of objections. This can happen to individuals in a variety of contexts, personally, socially, in their team or organization. In many cases the reason why this happens is through other people's fear of the unknown, lack of understanding, refusal to move from the *status quo*.

Equally some responsibility has to be taken by the individual in their reluctance to share their ideas, hopes, dreams or aspirations. Knowing when to share an idea is difficult, embryonic ideas are like delicate pieces of glass prior to assembly in a stained glass window. If the ideas are shared too soon it is as if a hammer is brought down shattering the idea into a thousand pieces. If the ideas are shared into a nurturing environment they can be cleaned, polished and perhaps turned slightly so that they make an even better picture. Here the analogy can be extended and likened to completing a very large jigsaw; sometimes because the task is so big, having help in finding a particular piece can bring people together, however the master wants to fit the final piece themselves (see Stephanie Oerton Case Study, Chapter 9).

In organizations like Disney where there is displayed thinking, people can share their embryonic ideas, and can have their idea added to, improved or developed by others. As discussed in Chapter 4, Mavericks may not want to implement all the ideas that they generate. Other like-minded people can take ideas on and develop them. Having a trusted sounding board and supportive teams can be invaluable.

Often if an idea fails the individual is sent to the equivalent of Siberia and as a result ideas are not properly reviewed either as part of the evaluation process, or as part of monitoring of success. All that is recorded is that it didn't work, but not why. This is why it is important to recognize the six stages of the innovation process (see Chapter 1).

Organizationally the 'naysayers' as Goleman would describe them have very long memories.

Against this backdrop it is critically important to focus on how to combat both the 'deadening effect' as Peter Honey describes in his Case Study (Chapter 9) of some organizations and to find a way of supporting all individuals whether they are in a school, a further/higher education establishment, or a corporate environment. Many of the respondents in the questionnaire and those interviewed cited examples of how organizations either don't recognize talent, or choose to stifle those who appear to be outside the accepted 'norm'.

What causes the 'deadening effect'? What happens to people as they move up an organization? Why is it, after the comparative billions that organizations have spent over the years with consulting firms, after the millions of words that have been written in books, or in research papers that we do not have a solution to the question of how to create a great organization?

So how do you channel the creative talents of individuals?

The people who responded to the Maverick questionnaire and the case studies have some excellent advice for how organizations can stimulate creativity (see Chapter 7).

In *Organizing Genius: The Secrets of Creative Collaboration,* Bennis and Biederman explore the concept of Great Groups. They believe that the organizations of the future will 'increasingly depend on the creativity of the members to survive'. In their case studies of seven Great Groups they identified some critical factors about how talented people work together. In their summary of the lessons learned from their study they suggest the following about recruiting talented people:

> 'Recruiting the most talented people possible is the first task of anyone who hopes to create a Great Group. The people who can achieve something truly unprecedented have more than enormous talent and intelligence. They have original minds. They see things differently. They want to do the next thing, not the last one... Great groups are headed by people confident enough to recruit people better than themselves. They revel in the talent of others... Being part of a group of superb people has a profound effect on each member... Participants know that their inclusion is a mark of their own excellence... People in Great Groups are always stretching because of the giants around them... Great Groups always believe they are doing something vital, even holy.'

Individuals have far more talent then we give them credit for; time after time we hear comments about workers who leave their brains at the door of their organization because they won't be needing them until they leave to go home to be a parent, or member of the community.

Creating a coaching environment

One major way of helping all individuals flourish is to develop a coaching environment; this is not something that will be achieved overnight, but if you can engender a sense of sharing wisdom you are more likely to create a real sense of personal development. This is very different from the process of 'managing', and is something that many of the respondents to the questionnaire wanted (see Chapter 4).

A coach guides rather than manages; throughout history there have been instances of guidance being given by 'elders'. What if instead of creating 'managers' we created guides? What if we gave respect to the wisdom of our experienced workers? The very best supervisors and managers are those who share their wisdom and give guidance to new employees. The very worst managers are those who play it by the rules with no flexibility, or explanation.

Individuals need to think about their very best learning experiences, to remember what inspired them, to think about how they can recreate special learning. Managers need to forget about being in control, instead helping their team members to explore by asking open questions and being provocative; and although individuals should never be taken unsupported outside their comfort zone, they can be encouraged to push their boundaries beyond their normal learning experiences.

Traditionally, coaching was something that might have only been offered to senior executives, or fast track employees. However, as more and more people become aware of the benefits of one-to-one support, coaches may be found operating at a number of levels within an organization. Another major advantage is that if people really begin to adopt coaching behaviours the organization becomes much more of a learning environment. People really do start to learn from each other, but it needs attention to survive, and this is one of the major challenges: in any large organization it takes constant attention to maintain any initiative. Too many employees are introduced to an idea, process, and way of working, only to find that it is not sustained. (See *Personal Coaching, Releasing Potential at Work* by Kaye Thorne.)

Creating the right environment for learning

Most memorable learning experiences usually take place in a special environment. By recreating the sensation of that special environment learners can apply the lessons learnt to different situations. This very much links to the concept of 'flow' (see Chapter 3); by remembering the sensation of special learning events it may be possible to enhance other learning situations.

One of the questions in the study was 'Thinking back over your learning experiences, how do you prefer to learn?' The responses naturally reflect the different learning styles that one would expect in a sample of individuals, but a high proportion of the respondents prefer to learn through doing or, as Kolb might describe it, 'active experimentation'. In the same way, Ian Banyard (see his Case Study) describes learning before you go to school, 'kids just make it up, they experiment, if one way doesn't work they try another, school teaches them about failing, not just in the task, but personally'.

In the survey, not just in response to this particular question, individuals cited the importance of their conversations with others either as a sounding board, or with someone who was like-minded who could help them explore their ideas further, adding to their picture, or reshaping certain aspects of it. This also reflects the way that many people prefer to learn, discovering with others rather than being told the facts by a specialist. What is important, as with a number of other aspects of the survey, is the need for feedback: even though individuals may want to learn through discovery they also want to know how well they are doing and to have access to coaching when they need it.

How do people prefer to learn?

Here is a summary of some of the responses from the survey:

Actively, learning through experience, hands on, with time for reflection.

I guess by accident! I really like it when learning happens by 'osmosis' – an almost accidental transfer of data that enables me to 'connect' apparently disconnected stuff together and create alchemy. I dislike formal education and anyone that portrays themselves as a 'specialist'. Conversations tend to please me more than lecturers and teachers.

By doing/physically engaging with an issue or idea. In terms of Kolb's learning styles I am an 'activist'.

In at the deep end, on the job and under pressure from the outset! But need regular new challenges, and prone to challenging established systems and procedures.

Alone in a research-based way, ie give me the topic and I'll do the work, just be there to answer questions.

By experimenting. I like to 'get on and try it'. Then, I want someone to help me by coaching. Finally, I want someone to praise me for doing it really well.

Definitely by doing – I can read manuals, I can listen and absorb but being shown and being allowed to try are my favourites.

Personally, I learn a lot through reading and reflecting.

A – Learning practical tasks – By doing something; by 'acting the part'; watching and 'imaging' how the person is responding, eg I tried to learn golf by imaging how Lee Trevino might do it (didn't get too far).

B – Ideas/processes/intellectual things – get the basic principle first then bounce off others – challenge the status quo; use 'devil's advocate' approach; deliberately taking things literally and seeing where it goes.

C – New ideas/problem solving – often after a thought has been bubbling around in the head for days/weeks/months; often when I should be doing something else but the thing I'm doing sparks an insight. If I have time

---

(permission?) to follow it, there can be progress and learning. Especially good with B above.

I learn by doing or seeing – it must be active to stick.

In a flexible, part-time, way, eg get a bit of theory, practise a bit, go away to let it sink in and connect with the real world, reflect, come back, try some more. Also, get multiple perspectives – hear other people – try something in different ways – different scenarios. Without too fixed an agenda, to allow exploration, but with a purpose in mind too.

On my own, rather than in a classroom environment, where I can dictate the pace.

I prefer to learn by the process of observation – watching and listening. I believe, and have always believed, that every one with whom I interact has something to offer me in the form of learning. I rarely get into a judgmental mode.

By being involved and having a go, adjusting my style and ideas as I go along and learning which ways work best. And by looking back over the experience and reviewing the results.

I enjoy problem-based learning – being creative to solve a problem or satisfy a market need.
Learning by discovery – the sense of seeking out or stumbling across things. Considering 'what happens if…' scenarios that challenge assumptions.

Physical skills by observing demonstration and then practise with unobtrusive coaching.
Knowledge-based skills through text-based reading, tutor led examples and group work.

By 'doing' and learning from experience. I respond well by also having a mentor to bounce ideas off and to help me review what went well/badly.

A number of people in the case studies and in the responses to the questionnaire emphasized the competitiveness of their nature and this came through in some of the responses about learning:

By working with others aiming to achieve very high levels of performance.

By researching best practice… and then trying to better it!

Good at active experimentation – going where others fear to tread!
Learn from mistakes well.
Also like theory and time to reflect – often on trains, in car.
Learn from irrelevance as well as 'relevance'.

I prefer to be left to my own devices with occasional input from a tutor when absolutely necessary.

Active, active and active… and when I get something to read, ie not my preferred style, I skim read so much that I often miss the point!

By reading and experiencing without stress, or time pressure. I am an exam phobic!

By trying things out and making new connections. Insights usually from new pattern, or anomaly.

Hands-on, highly participative, clearly defined objectives.

What these responses show is that individuals do have differing learning styles. This is illustrated in Kolb's learning cycle in which he identifies the key steps in how people learn and defines them as follows:

Having an experience: Whether it is managing a project, giving a presentation or completing a development activity. Searching out new and challenging experiences, problems and opportunities. Finding like-minded people to learn with. Making mistakes and having fun.

Reviewing the experience: Reflecting on what went well and what could have been improved, as well as seeking feedback from others.

Standing back from events to watch, listen and think. Listening to a wide cross-section of people with varying views. Investigating by probing, assembling, and analyzing information. Reviewing what has happened, and what you have learned.

Theorizing about what happened and why, then exploring options and alternatives: Questioning and probing logic and assumptions. Exploring ideas, concepts, theories, systems and models. Exploring interrelationships between ideas, events and situations. Formulating your own theories or models.

Planning what to do differently next time: Finding out how the experts do it. Looking for practical applications of ideas. Finding opportunities to implement or teach what you learn. Trying out and practising techniques with coaching and feedback.

It is important to recognize that not all learning may take place in a neat and ordered way. As a number of the respondents confirmed, we often learn best when we combine more than one approach to learning:

- Theory input

- Practical experience

- Application of theory

- Idea generation.

Kolb's learning cycle is also linked to the work of Honey and Mumford and their Learning Styles Questionnaire. See www.peterhoney.com. We all prefer to learn in slightly different ways:

- Activists learn best by doing.

- Reflectors learn best by observing.

- Theorists learn best by thinking things through in a logical and systematic manner.

- Pragmatists like to learn through putting their ideas into practice and testing them out.

Another expert on how we learn is Howard Gardner, a prominent psychologist who argues that everybody possesses at least seven intelligences. This information may be of particular interest to learners who want to have their senses stimulated when they learn, and in reviewing the answers from a number of respondents to the survey many of them use these intelligences when learning. Find out more in Gardner's book *Frames of Mind*. The following list is based on and adapted from research by Howard Gardner:

1. *Linguistic intelligence* – the intelligence of words, these learners will usually prefer learning from books, tapes, lectures and presentations.

2. *Logical-mathematical intelligence* – the intelligence of logic and numbers, these learners will usually prefer learning by creating and solving problems, playing mathematical games.

3. *Musical intelligence* – the intelligence of rhythm, music and lyrics. These learners will usually learn by using music, may use rhymes to help remember.

4. *Spatial intelligence* – the intelligence of mental pictures and images, uses symbols, doodles, diagrams and Mind Maps® to learn.

5. *Bodily-kinesthetic intelligence* – the intelligence of expression through physical activities, learns through doing, taking action, writing notes. Need frequent breaks when learning.

6. *Interpersonal intelligence* – the intelligence of communicating with others, they learn from others, like learning in teams, comparing notes, socializing, teaching.

7. *Intrapersonal intelligence* – the intelligence of self-discovery, they learn by setting personal goals, taking control of their learning, reflecting on their experiences.

If we review what the respondents to the questionnaire said about learning we see the following words:

> 'Active involvement, on-going coaching, lots of praise, positive feedback, conversations, time to reflect, things which come out of a clear blue sky, in at the deep end, by experimenting. Get on and try it, then help me by coaching, finally I want someone to praise me for doing it really well. Active, active, active.'

Learning is one of the most individual and personal activities that we ever undertake and yet most of us do most of our learning lumped together in environments that give us very little opportunity for individual coaching and support. For creative and innovative people, whatever their age, this is even harder. They crave feedback, they need time to reflect, they want very specific coaching to help them develop what they know they need to know. Unlike many others they often have a purpose to their learning and they get incredibly frustrated with what they may perceive as trivia or irrelevant information.

What is also very relevant is that if a learner enjoys the learning experience they are more likely to learn and remember. If they are told they need to learn something, their willingness to learn will depend on the respect that they have for the person telling them and their desire to learn. In order to create meaningful learning experiences, teachers, lecturers, trainers, workplace coaches and individual learners could do so much more to develop effective learning patterns. Ironically much pre-school and early years learning does focus on more stimulating ways of learning, unfortunately much of the opportunity to experience learning properly seems to disappear as individuals progress through school and career.

Moving from the 'little boxes'

What is so sad is that, given the responses above and the examples in Chapter 3 and Chapter 4 about creativity and inspiration, organizations continue to create working and learning environments which are so lacking in inspiration. Reading the responses in the earlier chapters and in this chapter it is clear that people want and need better working environments. A number of people in our case study examples have made lifestyle choices about where they work and live. We know through the work of Paul Torrance, David Kolb, Honey and Mumford, Daniel Goleman, Ricardo Semler, and Howard Gardner that people respond positively to different learning stimuli, and yet most corporate environments strip out the senses and some of our city universities are concrete prisons where lecturers struggle with their own motivation let alone trying to inspire their students.

When we are on a beach in the summer we often lazily look to the sky and see a small plane with a banner trailing behind advertising some local event; imagine a similar plane travelling over the top of many organizations with the statement, 'Wave your hand if you would rather be somewhere else'. What response would you expect? Unfortunately I anticipate the response would be a sea of waves. We have so much work to do to help organizations, whether they are schools, further or higher education, or places of employment, become somewhere that individuals enthusiastically want to attend.

We **must** think about doing it differently and celebrate those schools, colleges and organizations where real progress has been made in either ways of working, environment, or in giving individuals freedom to be themselves.

CHAPTER 6

Innovation and enterprise behaviours

Small can be beautiful

In the last decade there was a huge explosion in the setting up of SMEs which have been courted by numerous business support agencies, both governmental and in financial services. The growth of the entrepreneur, the owner manager, the self-employed, the sole trader has had a significant impact on the economy and the pattern of employment for many. Within industry, businesses have tried to develop the concept of 'intrapreneur', the idea of bringing small business principles into large organizations. Indeed, there has also been a growth of new businesses that have developed and grown from small start-up businesses.

There are some important lessons to be learned from small businesses:

- The passion and energy to start something new

- The commitment to make it happen

- The desire to create new ways of working

- The care and compassion for other members of the team

- The belief in the product or service

- The willingness to work hard to make it a success.

However, as a small business starts to grow there are often issues about how to manage the success. Ben Finn (see Case Study, Chapter 9) explains how critical it is to recruit the right people and that sometimes it is better to run the business a little longer with less people than to recruit the wrong people. Llorett Kemplen also describes the challenge of innovating ideas on your own after working within a supportive team environment (also Case Study). Often the skill set required is very different; this is particularly true for a sole trader that wants to grow, or for a small group.

Trying to attract the right kind of funding – trying to explain your exciting new concept to financiers who do not necessarily understand your business and who are rarely excited by an idea, preferring to see hard evidence in a business plan – is challenging at best and dispiriting at worst. What is needed is the best combination of creative and business minds who can work together to bring the best ideas to market. Where creative people have succeeded it is often because they have got the best advice, or have created teams of people who can help them translate their dream into reality.

Even within large businesses there is a recognition of the value of small business units. Jack Welch, the former CEO at General Electric (GE), is legendary in his approach to running an organization. Jack's goal in pushing for a learning culture, in driving quality, in transforming GE into a more service orientated enterprise, demonstrates that a multi-business company can endure and flourish. He believes that the benefits of having so many businesses outweigh the disadvantages, and GE's 12 major businesses do learn from each other. At a time when other organizations were attempting to focus on only a few core businesses, Welch saw the advantages in owning a diverse set. 'What sets GE apart is a culture that uses this wide diversity as a limitless store of learning opportunities,' he explains 'at the heart of this culture is an understanding that an organization's ability to learn, and translate that learning into action rapidly, is the ultimate competitive business advantage.'

It seems that one of the issues is size and how to grow incrementally. The size and growth of an organization can impact on a number of critical factors: communications, recruitment, day-to-day operations, decision making, style of management and ultimately business success. As mentioned elsewhere, there needs to be as short a line as possible between those taking the decisions and those implementing them.

In organizations with a long chain of command and several layers of management it is virtually impossible for real information to reach those who need to take the decisions. One of the well-known sayings about royalty is that the only smell they know when meeting the public is that of fresh paint; it is often similar with senior executives: when they visit the shop-floor, or the sharp end of the business, they are only told what people believe they want to hear. Talk to training consultants who train middle management and they will tell you the common comment is, 'Are our senior managers coming on this course?' or, 'We would do it, but it's our managers that stop us'. The only way of breaking the cycle is to bring the various groups together. Bill Legg (see Case Study, Chapter 9) gave a similar comment, '… any big company is effectively run by middle management, a fact lots of organizations overlook, although the strategy and policies are set by senior management it is the guys in the middle who are caught between trying to interpret and implement the policies of senior management and persuading those working in the engine-room of the company that it is the right thing to do.'

CEOs must be as accessible as possible; we must remove the barriers and the mystique of leadership. CEOs and senior management must be coached and given feedback on how to talk not just to their employees, but also to their shareholders and the media. We must take away the 'Emperor's New Clothes' syndrome, we must allow employees to say the unthinkable. This does not mean anarchy and importantly it does not mean taking away respect, but respect is a two-way street: organizations that do not treat their employees fairly or with respect cannot expect respect back from their employees.

It also means that organizations should support those who struggle to change, but ultimately both the employees and the organization need to recognize the dilemma of those required to change wherever they are in the organization. It is not an age or role issue, it is a behavioural issue; some people find it very difficult to change their behaviour, particularly if throughout their working life they have never received feedback on their style of management.

If the role models around you have shown you, or told you, to manage in a particular way, then you will find it hard to adapt to a different style of management, and internal communications literature, or impassioned speeches by the CEO, or even training courses are not going to help you change your behaviour.

You need all of that and coaching on top, and even then it may prove too difficult for some people; and that is when the real challenges start to come in.

Who will be brave enough to recognize that some members of the board need to leave? Who will have the courage to remove a high performing regional director who rules by fear and appears to get results? Who is around to hear the individual performance reviews when real talent is being stifled by managers who feel threatened by individual team members? How many creative thinking 'nu-joins' stay around long enough to recognize that there are other people like them in the organization, and that there is an opportunity for them to develop their talents?

How much real notice is taken of exit interviews and, as Andy Pellant suggests (Case Study, Chapter 9), how much real time is spent with new hires when they start with a company? If, as Andy suggests, a CEO spends three hours in a one-to-one conversation what a difference that would make to the individual's perspective of the company.

> 'Stop trying to believe that your power comes from what you know, and recognize that power comes from what you ask. Be remembered for the contact that you had with people, ask difficult, ask stupid questions. Ask your people what they would do if they were the MD. Spend three hours with a new hire within five days of their joining rather than talking to them as part of a crowd once a year. Create an obsession with nurturing people and diversity. Be extraordinary, it amazes me how CEOs do ordinary things and want to be thought extraordinary.'
>
> (Andy Pellant Case Study)

As Peter Honey recollects in his case study, having run a school with the headmaster he had no desire to return to being a student again.

A few years ago one of the words that seemed to be on everyone's lips was 'empower'. Like most pieces of jargon it got misinterpreted and ridiculed by many, but the concept behind it is sound; we do need to empower people, we do need to encourage everyone from the newest recruit to the most senior manager to use their initiative and to take action. Consumers and customers of every business large and small would have far less cause for complaint if the individuals they dealt with took more responsibility and did not hide behind bureaucracy, or the complaints procedure. It would eradicate the 'jobsworth' mentality.

A number of participants in the questionnaire and in the case studies mentioned the fact that it was their organization's need for control or power that stifled the innovation and creativity. Organizations like neatness and order, they like conformity, they struggle with people who are different, they feel threatened by change.

One way of overcoming this is to break the corporate hold by creating smaller communication cells. Essentially what this means is that communications are controlled through a powerful process of internal communication. This will take direct action at a number of levels and is based on the same organizational model as outlined in Chapter 4. The CEO and the executive board take decisions based on a process of feedback information from external sources about the state of the competition, the world markets and the performance of their own organization.

This information is used to shape and inform business strategies and policies within the organization. The overall highlights and non-sensitive information is shared with the workforce through the communication cells; the cells are large enough to be representative and small enough to allow informed discussion. There are opportunities for questions and every individual is encouraged to feel part of the process. Both those giving the message and those receiving it are shown respect, open behaviour is the norm, the normal courtesies in conversation are encouraged.

The cells continue to be a focus of communication by hosting regular opportunities to share information and to discuss business issues. Employees are asked for their views on new product development, feedback from customers, issues about current products or processes. As mentioned in Chapter 1, by focusing on the organization brand every organization has a ready source of key information about how the business is doing, why ignore it by being afraid of telling management what they may not want to hear?

This process of communication can be supported by clarity in job roles, 'SMART' (Specific, Measurable, Achievable, Realistic/Relevant and Timed) objectives and a clear understanding of what is needed to be done by each individual in order to meet the objectives. Many people who work for corporations are starved of information; they also often spend far too much time waiting for decisions to be taken. Even with the vast investment by many organizations in re-engineering, real action still takes far too long. Too many organizations still have outdated processes built on the premise that 'we have always done it like this'.

Why? Does it still need to be done like this? Who are we going to offend if we do it differently? Were we more efficient before we changed the process? Sometimes people are so afraid of admitting that the old way was better they stick with new processes even though they are less efficient, simply as a way of saving embarrassment. How much do we listen to feedback from employees, or our customers?

The reason why 'small' is so important is the ability to create dynamic working groups. Within this context the line of communications can be shorter and decisions made more quickly and more effectively. However, differences of opinion may be more apparent, emotions may be more volatile and there will be less opportunity for individuals to hide behind bureaucracy. Being self-employed, or working in a small organization does have real advantages for creative and innovative individuals. The freedom to work how and when you want and the ability to make things happen can be very attractive. One of the key issues for some individuals is the desire not to be responsible for managing others. In our survey a number of participants expressed a view that while they were 100% happy in managing themselves, they did not want to manage others. When questioned further the issues raised were as follows:

> 'When you are being creative you have to spend time on your own generating an idea or working out a solution, to then also have responsibility for managing others can dull your capacity to be spontaneous.' (See Chapter 4 for more responses.)

Some of the issues around management of others links to the style of management adopted by many organizations. Despite well reasoned arguments by Peters and Goleman amongst others, organizations still tend to develop their managers in very traditional ways.

GE and some of the younger businesses like Microsoft, Virgin, Dyson, Richer Sounds, espouse doing it differently, but talk to many individuals about the management style in their organization and you will find comments similar to those outlined in Chapter 7 (see *How organizations inhibit creativity and innovation*). One of the biggest issues for many large organizations is the structure of management. Despite tremendous advances in the technology, communications and other parts of the infrastructure of an organization, the style of management of people is often archaic. In the absence of progressive role models managers often manage in the way that they were managed, using a controlling model.

Why do people need managing?

Unfortunately managing as a concept conjures up a picture of individuals being herded like sheep, unable to take decisions, or to think for themselves and sadly many traditional organizations create environments where individuals are afraid of voicing an opinion, or sharing their independent thoughts. Against this backdrop it is difficult to stimulate not just innovative and creative people, but any individual into being proactive and acting on their own initiative.

We are living in unusual times. Tom Peters has for several years expressed the view that CRAZY TIMES CALL FOR CRAZY ORGANIZATIONS. We are still witnessing too many large organizations lumbering around like dinosaurs finding themselves in a 21st century landscape unable to move forward, bleeding and shaking their heads as they try to understand what has happened to their world. The prognosis is not good for those organizations who do not recognize that they have to change to develop, but more importantly to have a hope of surviving in the new business landscape.

How to change?

If you consider the scale and infrastructure of many of our large organizations it is not an easy task to achieve. To foster enterprise there is a need to understand what is meant by being entrepreneurial and to adopt measures that replace lugubrious actions with a fleetness of foot. From the top to the bottom of the organization there is a need to focus on key actions which make things happen, eg:

- clear decision making process
- effective communications
- create enterprise cells
- benchmark against others
- recognize what the competition is doing
- sense the value of being first
- recognize the potential to learn from being second
- acknowledge failure, but value the lessons learned from mistakes
- celebrate successes but do not become complacent
- evaluate, review and monitor progress
- be proud of achievements, but humble in glory
- be supportive of employees
- have commitment to your local community.

Being enterprising implies taking the initiative, being energized, making things happen and there is an assumption that this occurs in smaller organizations; however, small enterprises are not necessarily without their problems. If we refer to the Innovation 3® model (see

---

page 117), one of the very real issues in a small organization is how to address each stage. For a self-employed person or a small team, trying to cover all stages may not be possible. Using outside support may be necessary, but this could be on a consultancy or part-time basis. Another alternative is to pay a small fee for a very specific service from an outside agency.

Incrementally there are significant phases of growth, and the owner managers often find it requires different skill sets to manage and grow the business than it does to create and develop new ideas. Organizationally, the model of innovation illustrates how the different stages in the innovation process need people with different preferences and competencies.

Idea generators may not be the best people to implement the idea. Those who enjoy developing and exploring an idea may not be the best people to evaluate it. There are distinct differences in preference between those who prefer to work away from others and those who are more gregarious and who can develop network contacts, or spot linkages between other projects. Being entrepreneurial within a larger organization can have distinct advantages where individuals are encouraged to demonstrate enterprise behaviours within smaller working groups. However, to be really successful there still needs to be a process that recognizes the existence of such groups, and ways created where real responsibility is devolved to these groups.

There is a process of clear communications and decision making across the whole business. In this way it is possible to benefit from both small and large business processes. Some of the most well-known examples of this are in Semco, the Brazilian manufacturing company owned by Ricardo Semler, Richer Sounds in the UK owned by Julian Richer, Virgin owned by Richard Branson. At the Sibelius Group, a best-selling music notation software business, Ben and Jonathan Finn (Case Study, Chapter 9) are also working to develop progressive ways of managing individuals, but huge progress has to be made in our corporate organizations before real change occurs. This is one of the issues raised by Sheena Matthews, another of the case study participants, when she mentions the issues that can arise when you are working to achieve change and the organization recruits to type; she asks the question 'What messages does this send out to your employees about how serious you are about change?'

Yet traditional managers need support and help to change; some may not be able to achieve the level of change required. If during all your career you have been rewarded for demonstrating a particular style of behaviour, it is not enough simply to be told that you need to change; neither will it work if you are just sent on a course. To learn new behaviour you need much more: you will need to know what is expected of you, what new behaviours you need to demonstrate and ongoing coaching to help you practise, develop and demonstrate your competence. This required change of behaviour also needs to be set into an organizational context where the rationale and need for change is transmitted positively to the workforce and the need for support is shared with everyone. Changing a culture is an enormous task and it needs ongoing support if any level of success is to be achieved.

The six-stage model of innovation

Some years ago as part of a process called Innovation 3® I developed a six-stage model of innovation. This model builds on the stages of creativity, but recognizes some of the organizational behaviours which are designed to support the innovation process.

There are definite differences in an individual's preferences within the innovation process. Creative individuals have an important role to play but their inventive ideas will often only be fully implemented with the support of others – often by those who would describe themselves as not being creative. Everyone has a role to play in the generation and implementation of ideas. This is an area of critical importance for both individuals and organizations, as it is important to explore the reasons why some very creative and innovative people never fully exploit their potential. By understanding individual preferences and the preferences of others, teams and organizations can work more effectively together.

As you look at the six-stage model of innovation it is important to recognize the different stages of innovation and individual preferences. The logic is as follows:

Creating the climate

If the organization does not encourage and foster innovation, then it is likely that creative and innovative individuals will not feel able to make a full contribution. Importantly, within this context, is the willingness to give people personal space to be innovative.

One of the classic examples of this is 3M, mentioned above, who allow employees personal time to develop new projects; the precise time taken is not important – it is the principle of people being allowed time and space. Innovative organizations have an energy; they create open areas where people communicate and share ideas. Organizations like Disney use 'displayed thinking' where questions and development stories are shared with all employees. The Disney Institute runs an 'Imagineer It' programme which is designed to showcase the three phases an idea moves through from conception to implementation. It specifically highlights how Imagineers cultivate dreams, communicate designs, connect the talents of diverse builders and celebrate the new creation. It also plays to individual preferences; some managers make excellent facilitators and as such are able to help create the environment where innovation flourishes, while others are more comfortable with closer management.

The Innovation 3® process

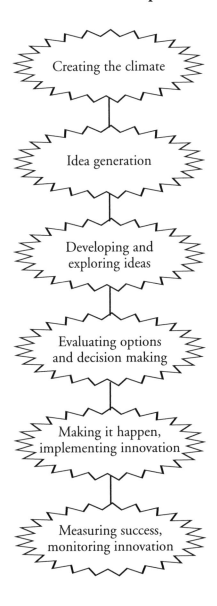

Creating the climate

Idea generation

Developing and
exploring ideas

Evaluating options
and decision making

Making it happen,
implementing innovation

Measuring success,
monitoring innovation

©The Inspiration Network

Idea generation

What makes some organizations able to innovate and others merely replicate is fascinating. There are many ways of addressing idea generation, but one of the most important is recognizing the fundamentals behind it, and the roles that different people can play. The organizations that really lead the field in innovation recognize how important it is to create the right climate, but also how to allow people to play to their strengths. For some people this may literally mean coming up with the good ideas, they are paid to think laterally; people expect them to suggest a number of ideas, some never see the light of day, some may be destined for failure, but their ability from time to time to come up with a 'winner' secures their organization's faith in them.

What the really innovative organization will do is put this 'originator' of ideas with a 'modifier' who will work together to originate and develop the overall concept.

Developing and exploring ideas

The overall concept does not stop there; building on this initial stage, the idea then goes into incubation where more people become involved and the idea is further developed. Teams may build on the original concept and start exploring linkages with other projects; presentations may be made to senior management. This stage needs to be handled very carefully; if the ideas and concepts are not explained clearly, the idea may be vetoed simply because those not involved in the initial process cannot grasp the concept. This is where it is important to have a balanced team of presenters who are able to tune into their audience. The difficulty often arises when people heavily involved in idea generation burst into someone's office exclaiming 'We've just discovered this new way of doing things' only to be given a frosty reception from those outside the creative process. Sharing concepts and ideas needs to be carefully planned, but it is also important to foster an environment which encourages experimentation and allows ideas to be evaluated non-judgementally. It also acknowledges that an 'initiator' may prefer to work on their own, while a 'builder' really needs others to share their ideas with. Mavericks often prefer to work on their own, and rarely want responsibility for managing others (see Chapter 4).

Evaluating options and decision making

One of the interesting facts about innovation is that anyone can come up with a good idea; however what really matters is taking a good idea and making it work. Coupled with this is the ability to identify the right idea and process it through to implementation. It is at this stage that some 'exploring' creative people can cause confusion. There are those people who cannot resist putting another spin on an idea. For example, a decision has been made about launching a product in the UK marketplace, the logo and name have been chosen, when someone says 'Actually I think this product would go better in France' and they begin to build a very persuasive argument. For the rest of the group, who were ready to go ahead on the UK option, this can be destabilizing, particularly if they respect the view of the person raising the question. Understanding the process and respecting each other's needs is very important. Equally, understanding when it is important to make a decision and to move forward is a discipline that some individuals and organizations lack. A common criticism levelled in these circumstances internally is 'We are very good at generating ideas, but we are less effective at following the idea through to successful implementation'. Having an effective process of evaluation is something that both individuals and organizations may find more of a challenge.

Making it happen, implementing innovation

This is the next critical stage in the process. At this point another part of the team may be involved. Often those responsible for idea generation may have less desire actually to implement the idea; it usually involves a different set of competencies. However, it is vitally important that the hand-over from one stage to the next is carefully engineered. If not, it will disenfranchise the designers from the implementers. This is one of the classic issues in many organizations where those responsible for generating the vision are different from those delivering it and there is a breakdown in the communication process. At this stage it is important both to plan for the implementation of the innovation, as well as actually implementing it.

Measuring success, monitoring innovation

Measuring success and monitoring innovation often requires the most discipline in an innovative organization. It is necessary to keep adequate records of the process, eg details of the key people involved, what the overall objectives were, how they were met, target audience, what changes were made and the overall outcome. In reality, the only way to capture this data effectively is to build it into the overall plan and to give the responsibility for data capture to an individual or team. Critically, however, it should be reviewed at the end of the project. Instead of rushing ahead with the next idea, it is important to ensure that the lessons learned are captured and that one idea is not dropped in favour of another for no good reason. Having people prepared to champion and sponsor ideas is an essential part of any organization's development. At this stage there will be those who are more able to see the co-ordinating links between the proposed innovation and other parts of the organization or external connections – they will often be expansive and celebratory in their comments. Others will have a more controlling preference and are less likely to acknowledge success until the innovation has been in place for some time, and may be less likely to wait for the innovation to succeed before closing it down.

The implication of this model is that individuals and organizations have a tool to identify the key stages and the individual preferences at each stage and thus teams can be assembled which play to individual strengths. It can also help in acknowledging differences. The Innovation Preference Inventory and the Organization Readiness Indicator (which are part of the Innovation 3® products, now managed by Enterprising Futures, TDA Transitions Ltd; please contact vmdunn@tdatransitions. co.uk for more details) allow people to understand both the process and their preferences.

People who find it difficult to share their ideas with others will find it particularly difficult working with individuals who are either high evaluators or high controllers, and to a certain extent high explorers because for solo idea generators the issue is about how and when to share ideas. If they share the idea spontaneously they may find that others ignore it or ridicule it, so many people do not share their ideas for fear of the criticism of others. They also may just leave an organization and take their creativity with them. In our survey a high proportion of people have chosen to work for themselves. This has potentially serious implications for both organizations and individuals. Equally, in using the Innovation Preference Inventory, individuals have often expressed a preference for either the inner circle of idea generation, developing, exploring ideas, evaluating options and decision making, or the outer organizational circle of creating the climate, making it happen/implementing innovation and measuring success/monitoring innovation. By helping people accommodate their preferences and letting them play to their strengths organizations could improve the effectiveness of their innovation process.

CHAPTER 7

Organizational innovation and creativity

The generation of an innovation culture is seen as one of the most critical areas of focus for organizations in the 21st century. Really successful organizations do not simply innovate; they accelerate and innovate again. Often the best ideas are developed in organizations that have created a process for idea generation: the Disney 'Imagineer It' programme, the Richer Sounds 'good idea' philosophy, are just two examples. This chapter will examine how organizations innovate and how to measure an organization's readiness for innovation.

What makes an organization great?

This is not just about innovation, it is also about how organizations grow and develop into being serious contenders in the marketplace. As discussed in Chapter 1 our business norms are changing, but in many ways not fast enough. Why are so many traditional businesses failing?

Often it is the result of clinging on to past successes and not recognizing the important but subtle changes in the marketplace. People are the lifeblood of any organization, ignore them at your peril; as a result of losing the heart and soul of your organization energies get dissipated, people's self-belief wobbles, leaders become arrogant or entrenched, partnerships with suppliers break down and the organization loses its belief in itself. When this happens the organization starts on a downward spiral and it takes a brave person to push for innovation. Building and sustaining a great business takes rare talent and unfortunately too few people achieve it.

And yet running a business is still based on a comparatively simple premise:

Great Products, Great Prices delivered with Great Service by Great People

Advances in global processes, technology and distribution haven't changed the basis of the offer and any business, great or small that wants to succeed still needs to be able to deliver against the same measure. The cause of failure of many great organizations can often be traced back to ignoring one or more parts of the basic offer.

However for those who aspire to greatness here are some important guidelines:

1. Be committed to developing an organizational brand.

2. Create a climate for innovation.

3. Use every opportunity to stimulate and generate good ideas.

4. Develop a process for evaluating, giving feedback and giving recognition for good ideas.

5. Encourage individuals to play to their strengths, develop trust and positive support for good ideas, encourage realistic and constructive

feedback, have enough openness to ensure that good ideas are not stifled but are evaluated effectively.

6. Benchmark and develop an overview, ensure co-ordination between different parts of the business.

7. Work to keep the organization alive and vibrant, take away the 'Emperor's New Clothes' syndrome.

8. Open up the lines of communication, create small empowered groups.

9. Leaders should be accessible, policies should make sense to employees and customers.

10. There should be the shortest possible distance between the leader and the led.

If you want to assess your organization's ability to foster innovation you may like to find answers to the following questions:

- Is there top management support?

- Do we champion idea generation?

- Do we accept ideas that break organizational precedent?

- Do we encourage cross-fertilization of ideas and perspective?

- Do we give people personal space to be creative?

- Do we tolerate failure in the pursuit of a good idea?

- Are changes in direction accepted as necessary?

- Do we reward ideas that develop business success?

Innovative organizations have energy; they create open areas where people can communicate and share ideas.

Characteristics of innovative organizations

- Nurture creativity

- Supportive but challenging

- Develop effective teamwork

- Encourage cross-company communication and co-ordination

- Support innovation

- Recognize small changes

- Allow time for reflection, debate

- Encourage active participation and involvement

- Create a climate of co-operation and trust.

How organizations inhibit creativity and innovation

One of the questions in the Maverick questionnaire focused on the actions that organizations take which inhibit creativity and innovation; here are a sample of the responses:

Doesn't have time to review ideas or recognize contributions, communication across multi-sites inhibits flow through.

Expects me to do things between 9 and 6.

Banking, I feel is rigidly legislated and regulated (probably correctly so). As such the industry does not itself spawn creative people (hugely generalistic I know).

Currently this question does not apply as I work for myself. In the past, however, organizations have constrained me because my ideas were 'not in the business plan' or seen as 'strategic imperatives'. Condemning failure also inhibits risk taking and creativity.

I guess my difficulties are:

- *Sticking to a narrowly defined role*
- *Persuading others of the value of my ideas.*

I hope nothing. I have recently set up a new company!

Heavy performance and delivery focus leaves less free time.

Spreads fear. Keeps making people redundant for no obvious reason + there is a very authoritative and anal CEO who always thinks of all the reasons why something will not work, when what you need is encouragement.

I work for myself, so only have myself to blame!

There is not currently a support staff… to handle some of the routine tasks that take away creative time.

I no longer work for an organization. When I did the inhibition to creativity was primarily about a real reluctance to try something unless you could prove in advance that it was a great idea. So, no sense of prototyping of processes, ideas, procedures or even things.

Makes us work so damn hard.

Uses creative people in inappropriate ways – after conception; involvement during gestation and being present at the birth is good – but not necessarily getting into the detail of doing it.

Some individuals can have a tendency to 'hijack' ideas for personal progression/promotion.

Classifies people too easily as 'creative' and 'uncreative'; and compounds this by assuming that marketing people are more creative than technical people.

Devalues the term 'brainstorms' by meetings that have this title, but not this aim, eg a project leader will know the preferred outcome but wants to use the session to enrol the team into their view of how the world should be. Calling these 'selling meetings' would be more honest and productive.

Builds long processes with lots of stage gates/approval committees etc.

This is a hybrid of lots of organizations that I have known!

- *Tries to define behaviours that will produce creativity and innovation*
- *Doesn't trust people*
- *Makes work serious, and creativity light interludes*
- *Makes creativity personal and innovation business like*
- *Lets people wander too far on their own – doesn't try to put some disciplines on the Mavericks (eg deadlines, asking for output)*
- *Doesn't differentiate between exploration and focus, eg apparently makes a decision, then allows it to be changed a short while later*
- *Talks a lot – walks less.*

Interruptions from clients – but that's par for the course.

Sometimes scared to make decisions. Sometimes lacks the conviction to dive in and make a decision, make it work and succeed whereas takes the approach of thinking and talking too long and misses the opportunities.

As a rule, creativity and thinking is not recognized as a skill, even though it's on my CV.

Focus on short-term goals and fear of failure.

I am very lucky that now I work for myself so I pretty much control what I do when. Previous to this I worked for an organization where I held a fairly senior position and again I was also allowed to do what I felt was right, when and where I liked. They were a very supportive innovative organization.

Natural instinct to (over) analyze.
Doesn't recognize and reward creativity and innovation.
Talks about it but doesn't live it.

A culture of blame stifles creativity.
Some bureaucratic systems don't help.

An emphasis on consensus (possibly linked to the blame culture) can mean the best result doesn't always happen (the camel-is-a-horse-designed-by-committee syndrome).

Promotes in its likeness, is risk averse, values what is right less than what is expedient or politically correct, fires Mavericks and promotes the safe and unimaginative.

They have recently introduced more processes that stifle creativity and innovation.

Direction from US without always understanding that there are different needs for different markets.

Lacks resources. Restricts freedom. Insists that the office/desk is where work is done – high level of stress. Sees innovation as a threat to the status quo.

Give me ten pages! Autocracy, fear and stress based on an arrogance rather than confidence. Working culture which does not permit responsibility and where decisions drift to too senior a level. Controlling, risk averse, blaming, avoids confrontation. Control subordinates and yield to superiors.

Upward blandification, do more of the same.

Operates as a traditional, hierachical, functional bureaucracy.

What does your organization do to stimulate creativity and innovation?

In contrast I also asked 'What does your organization do to stimulate creativity and innovation?'; here are a sample of the replies:

Promotes creativity and innovation through company values – its an expectation!
Encourages freedom and risk taking.

I am my organization and I do whatever I need to do. Creativity and innovation is what pays the bills and makes life interesting.

Leaves me alone!

Flat structure (so junior people can make suggestions to senior people).

Since the merger, greater opportunity has been given to people seeing 'outside the box' so that problems and processes are seen from different perspectives, enabling a more customer driven organization. After all, what are we without the customer? (Unemployed!!).

Empowers me to go out and make mistakes.
Others, which worked really well, include:
- *Building a team of creative people and empowering them to manage as a team; holding regular planning sessions (½ day every 2 weeks) with target-related outcomes*
- *Having creative leaders and role models within the organization*
- *Having the organization VALUE AND REWARD creativity.*

Creates the right environment for me.

Great use of brainstorms and some quality development teams. Employs great people.

Lets me get on with it.

Allows me to take on a zillion different roles with a supported independence.

Supports the idea if it fits in with the overall plan of the moment, shares the energy of enthusiasm and 'go for it' response.

It was a very, very open organization in allowing me to get away with doing what I wanted as long as I could demonstrate a track record of success.

OK, it also stimulates, permits us to come up with ideas (and celebrates them, too), has managers who understand creative folks, and generally creates a great climate! OK, so I like where I work. So?

Brainstorming – using a variety of techniques; involving a good mix of people (allows those who have been thought of as 'uncreative' to have a go). Encourages 'permissive' environment – flexible working; stimulating environments dedicated to brainstorming.

It does try to give people a fair degree of autonomy in the job.

Gives people the freedom to think.

Trains people in creative problem solving and facilitation.
Helps people to understand themselves.
Talks to real customers to find the unexpected. Ignores customers too, to produce things customers didn't know they needed.
Wanders around aimlessly.
Talks targets and then delivers on the promises.
Challenges people.

It enables flexible working.

Lets people be autonomous, as long as I continue to exceed the corporation's and my region's expectation I know they will give me complete flexibility.

My organization allowed me to take my team out of the business for a meeting every month, usually at a team member's house. Once every quarter we had a 'QC' (quaint cottage) which we rented on a self-catering basis somewhere in the Cotswolds or alike and both of these opportunities gave the team time to bond, generate ideas and get motivated.

Sits teams in open bays to encourage bonding and spontaneous communication.

Encourages experiment.
Gives people plenty of rope.

People have the freedom to take risks and try new things:
- *Expectation is that people will continually strive to be innovative*
- *Recognizes and rewards creativity.*

Freedom to experiment and trust in my judgements.

Some of the time, it leaves me to get on with the job – trusts me.

Go for swim.
Play in jam sessions.
Drinking.

They did reward creativity and innovation by awarding certificates and one-off payments but the criteria for these awards has now been widened to take in any extra effort made by the employees and this has taken away the value of the awards for creativity and innovation.

Zippo... nay the reverse is true. It hinders it... it pooh poohs it. It doesn't revel in it.

Devolution, encourage autonomy, tries to celebrate achievement.

A high tolerance of Mavericks, oddly enough it doesn't censure their ideas. Has think-tanks of bright young people. Supports me in setting up of challenge groups, face-to-face and virtual.

Freedom, challenge, freshness etc, etc. Too much to list.

Work teams, autonomy (for me if not others). Personal development.

Provides an incredible working environment.

How do you foster innovation?

Traditionally if there is an area needing improvement, organizations set up a department or allocate responsibility for it to a particular individual. However, what ought to happen is that it should be integrated into the fabric of the organization. Good ideas shouldn't just come out of a department for innovation. They ought to be the lifeblood of an organization and like the circulatory system it ought to be encouraged to flow to every part. Blockages should be operated upon, if necessary with a by-pass, equally transplants may be needed to keep a healthy flow of ideas and the stimulus for innovation.

One excellent example of this takes place in General Electric. The former CEO Jack Welch commented, 'The biggest accomplishment I've had is to find great people. An army of them. They are all better than most CEOs. They are big hitters, and they seem to thrive here.' In an average year Welch met and directly interacted with thousands of employees, thus he was able to promote people from lower down the ranks, his view being 'What counts is what you deliver'. In every leader Jack is looking for 'E to the fourth power'. That is his term for people who have enormous personal energy, the ability to motivate and energize others. Robert Slater, author of *Jack Welch and the GE Way*, distils Jack's advice as follows, 'act like a leader, not a manager, use the brains of every worker, keep it simple, embrace change and fight bureaucracy.'

As discussed in Chapter 6, there are distinct advantages in adopting a small business operating style within a large organization. However, whatever the size of the organization it is the climate that ultimately determines how innovative an organization can be. In Chapter 1 the development of an employer brand was discussed. In real terms, unless the CEO and the executive are committed to the sponsorship of innovation it is unlikely that there will be real progress in the development of new ideas. Innovation cannot flourish in an organization that does not sponsor idea generation.

When I was developing the Innovation 3® products I used the following sample of six statements in my presentations to organizations:

- This organization gives people personal space to be creative

- This organization leads rather than follows its competitors

- This organization innovates, accelerates and innovates again

- This organization champions people who think differently

- Ideas are evaluated against their impact on the business

- We are an organization that others benchmark against.

Sample of statements from Innovation 3® Organization Readiness Indicator ©The Inspiration Network

What was interesting was that I often got the response, 'What if our organization isn't doing any of them?' In reality these statements represent some of the greatest challenges for organizations:

This organization gives people personal space to be creative

Many corporate organizations still struggle with the concept of giving individuals personal time and space. As discussed in Chapter 3, saying that you are leaving the building to go and think would be viewed as suspiciously like having time off to do what you want to do.

This organization leads rather than follows its competitors

The response to this is very interesting; there are times when it is advantageous not to be first. However, what is important is that an innovative company has a competitive strategy, and has the ability to stay ahead of the competition and this links to the next statement.

This organization innovates, accelerates and innovates again

The most creative and innovative organizations usually recognize the importance of staying ahead of the competition where it is important to do so, and in many ways are prepared to share some of their ideas as best practice because they are already working on the next level of innovation.

This organization champions people who think differently

This is often a real challenge. Many organizations find it difficult to accept people who are different, let alone championing them. Many of the comments in the Maverick questionnaire are evidence of this fact. People who are creative, innovative and particularly those who may be described as Mavericks, often have to work very hard at helping the organization to consider doing things differently. Even those given responsibility for helping the organization be more innovative, or charged with helping it change, often struggle against a tide of complacency or fear of the unknown.

Ideas are evaluated against their impact on the business

What is important in this statement is that ideas are rarely properly evaluated; this does not just apply to innovation but to a number of business processes. Objectivity, whether in terms of setting objectives, or in evaluating and qualifying a course of action is often lost in the everyday operational activity of an organization. As stated elsewhere, ideas are rejected sometimes before they are tested because the belief is that 'it won't work', or 'it didn't work last time so we won't try it again'. Having a proper process of evaluation can be invaluable in discovering why something didn't work, or equally why it did work, and should be an integral part of the innovation process.

We are an organization that others benchmark against

This links back to a number of the points raised in Chapter 1; it is about engendering pride in the organization. It is about being proud of both individual and organizational achievements, and being prepared to share best practice. It is less about the process of externally benchmarking, but more about the philosophy of encouraging everyone internally to respond to the question 'How could we do everything we do better?' as Jonathan Evans illustrates (see Case Study, Chapter 9).

What are the challenges for organizations?

Innovation is not easily handled in organizations; the very nature of the process threatens to bring change, and change implies doing it differently. Differently might mean ambiguity, uncertainty – many organizations are uncomfortable having to deal with what they don't know. Mavericks tend to thrive on change, they are much more uncomfortable with certainty. Certainty could equal boredom, trying to control innovation could be counter-productive. As William Coyne, Senior Vice President Research & Development, 3M noted (see Chapter 1) innovation is 'fuzzy'.

As mentioned earlier, corporate organizations trying to encourage innovation have comparatively few successful role models. Very few organizations have embraced the philosophy of innovate, accelerate and innovate again. There are far more examples of large companies who were innovative and then basked in their success before realizing that the competition were catching them up.

One model that could prove an interesting challenge is given opposite. Imagine if organizations adopted this approach in terms of organizational development:

Innovation

One third of their time was spent in fostering innovation, idea generation, being creative, thinking about the future and ways of doing it differently.

Implementation

Implementation – should be carefully planned, no assumptions should be made, there should be balanced teams of people who can plan as well as implement. Pragmatism should be matched with imagination. People should be encouraged to ask the difficult questions, 'Why are we doing this?' 'Why is this a good idea?' 'What would happen if we did nothing?' Equally, if the majority decides that it is a good idea then the minority should also support the implementation, having had opportunity to voice their concerns, rather than do everything they can to disrupt the project.

Investigation

One area that consistently people do less well in is monitoring success, identifying what is done less well, maintaining consistent delivery and

---

maintaining customer satisfaction. One fundamental area of complacency is ignoring customers. Customers often really do know what they want: the consumer of today is very savvy, consumer programmes on the television, articles in the press, the higher profile of 'consumerism' means that today's customer is much more discerning and will swop allegiances. Even financial services, which traditionally traded on the apathy and nervousness of their customers to shop around for a better deal, are now finding themselves being challenged by a much more competitive marketplace. Every large plc has found itself under threat and some have managed to adapt, but many – like a super-tanker – find it difficult to implement changes quickly enough.

Investigation should include internal and external analysis. There should be people responsible for following an implementation through and responding to the feedback. Successes should be celebrated – failures acknowledged, analyzed and lessons learned. In Chapter 8 the work of Edison and Einstein is discussed, and the number of times they experimented with an invention before it worked. What support would a young Einstein or Edison get today?

So how do organizations manage innovation?

1. Create an environment where good ideas are the philosophy of the whole company rather than just a few 'creatives'. Develop the 'spirit of enterprise'.

2. Recognize the innovation process and encourage teams to work together building on each other's strengths.

3. Encourage one or two specific individuals to take a proactive approach to idea generation.

4. Suspend overly critical judgement; instead, give evaluative and positive feedback to help the idea generator explore options and

choices for implementation. Far too many good ideas are lost because of overly critical judgement applied too soon.

5. Develop values of trust, integrity, freedom of spirit.

6. Encourage a climate of self-awareness, creating a learning environment where individuals are encouraged to find out how best to learn, their personality and details of other preference profiles.

7. Play to individual strengths within a team, not expecting those who generate the idea to implement it. However, create strong communication and feedback channels to ensure that the original concept is maintained.

8. Create a 'positive' feeling around the business – there is a saying that if you focus on crisis you will generate crisis. Encourage all employees to 'feel good' about the business; focus on their needs, focus on becoming an 'employer of choice'.

9. Create a coaching environment where line managers are encouraged to share learning and where knowledge and wisdom are valued.

10. Think about the emotional competencies of your employees, recognize the impact of increased awareness of personal and social competencies (see Daniel Goleman).

11. Develop a culture of using tools and techniques for innovation, encourage use of Mind Mapping®, Six Thinking Hats, displayed thinking, brainstorming.

12. Streamline processes for evaluation, decision making and feedback, thus increasing speed to market.

13. Champion people who think differently. Seek to be the organization that others benchmark against.

How can organizations nurture talent?

In the Mavericks questionnaire the last question I asked was as follows:

If you could change one aspect of organizations that would encourage the nurturing of talent, what would you recommend?

There was such wisdom and impassioned pleas that I have included a comprehensive summary of the responses below, together with some of the additional comments that individuals wanted to make:

Don't pooh, pooh the idea but try the idea…, don't think of why you can't do it… just do it.

It is better to have tried and failed than not to have tried at all.

Don't punish those that try and fail – praise and nurture.

I feel talent is something people are born with and therefore recognition should begin during their schooldays with a separate education stream/ qualification system which would carry through to the work environment where they could be on the promotion ladder but (as with my organization) categorized as individual.

The recognition that not everyone fits into a particular way of achieving a set goal.

Encourage trust and leave people to find themselves.

Establishing strong behavioural principles led by example-not-words from all leaders and, eventually, all employees.

I truly hope your research has an influence before we get even further behind the USA.

Senior managers being prepared to step outside their conventional modus operandi *and/or being prepared to tolerate and/or support others to do so.*

Create an extended order (after Hayek and Complexity theory) inspired by a few general principles, not detailed procedures which are outdated as soon as they are written.

Leadership needs to drive the harnessing of human talent – most companies don't have leaders that understand how to do this.

Flexibility – understanding that following the 'way we do things here' is a recipe for stagnation.

Recognition (not necessarily reward) for the value they deliver.

More honest feedback on a regular basis, to encourage and reinforce positive risk taking.

Let people work when and where they think they can offer the greatest potential, it always amazes me that more companies do not let their staff work from home now and again, so much more can be achieved and when they are away from the office and the confines of 'its' thinking, they can open their mind to thinking in other ways.

For people to be fully committed to giving their ideas to an organization who may make a million pounds from the idea, is probably a major area for discussion. If I had a great idea to save the company millions I could just as well go set up my own company, sell the idea and make the million for myself – how far will organizations be willing to go to keep the idea and the person who came up with it?

How are ideas given value and how is this value repaid to those who generated the idea? If the idea came in someone's sleep, when he/she wasn't being paid because he/she wasn't at work, how will this be valued or rewarded?

I can tell from my personal experience, the one thing that the organization must do to nurture talent is to provide challenge to the individual. Continuous challenge of the individual that stretches him/her to their wits end is the best 'mantra' to nurture talent in the organization.

In organizations, I believe, the maximum learning takes place when the boss is demanding. A demanding boss, creative people surrounding me and enabling organizational culture is the concoction that I recommend to foster creativity.

Having the flexibility of mind to explore new ideas without defending the old paradigm so completely.

If our organization isn't doing it, who is? – which is the great majority of British industry – not doing it, that is.

Japan has a far better approach to innovation and ITS ACCEPTANCE...

Stop thinking short term at the risk of mortgaging the longer term. But rather take short-term tactical actions that both move the business forward on a short-term basis but also in the context of where the business is heading longer term.

Yes, when one joins a company one is full of ideas and perceptions that one has from previous companies etc. In the first 48 hours these should be written down and sealed in an envelope. This has to be done in the first 48 hours before 'brainwashing occurs'! Then a month later the envelope should be opened and relevance/irrelevance should be examined.

Giving Mavericks a free rein runs the risk of alienating other managers who are not bracketed in that category. Like graduate and other high-flyer development programmes, there is almost a need to set up a separate internal channel to meet the needs of Mavericks. The business benefits of retaining the Mavericks should outweigh any additional administrative burden.

Perhaps a deeper issue is that organizations say they want to be more creative... but do they really? Creative people are often unmanageable loners, do you really want them in your organization; 90% of creative ideas are garbage, only 10% are actually worthwhile, do organizations really want their managers wasting 90% of their time? It's like putting on a play – which is 99% tedium of preparation and 1% exciting when you actually give the performance.

In my opinion, the real issue is: are organizations really prepared to employ Mavericks and be innovative… and endure all that that entails?

Mavericks and talent are not the same thing – everyone has talent but not everyone is a Maverick.

Key thing: make the process of being an employee a two-way relationship and contract. Employer lays out what they think they need in the way of outcomes, and suggested processes, and what they are willing to offer. Employee lays out what they want from the job experience, how they think they could contribute, and what they are willing to offer. Both sides have to take responsibility for their actions. Trouble with employers telling people what to do is that people feel they can blame the employers when it goes wrong. So, to be treated like individuals (which is what Mavericks often say they want) they have to take responsibility for what they do and the impact it has on everyone else – they can't expect to be left alone unless they don't want anything in return – like money or appreciation!

Keep management systems simple – the flow chart should fit on one side of A4 in a minimum 12 point font!

The appointment of a court jester to the CEO.

Encourage people to enjoy what they do and provide them with the possibility to enjoy what they do. I say 'encourage' and 'possibility' because you cannot impose enjoyment.

Reward on the basis of contribution to ideas AND results rather than on grade/project profile/targets alone.

Everyone is creative; everyone has a 'Maverick-streak'. An organization best utilizes this by recognizing how important such recognition is to that individual. There may not be a straight-line relationship between the 'degree of creativity' and the need to have this recognized. After a threshold, the need to express creativity may steeply rise then plateau and rise sharply again. If it is the only thing that gets someone out of bed in a morning, they should be carefully nurtured (or shown the door if it is inappropriate to the organization – hopefully a rare occurrence).

Values. Which is a form of belief. If you believe your people are creative, then guess what. You act that way. Then guess what, they act that way.

You must read Orbiting the Giant Hairball *by Gordon MacKenzie.*

Personal acclaim and recognition following achievements and results and it doesn't always need to be monetary!!

Remove hierarchical structures and promote co-operative practice only.

3½ day working week for full time money (we work too much).

Learning to listen, learning how to dialogue. Is that two?

Not overloading people with routine or administrative work. Giving them time to dream.

Acceptance of the need for continual positive challenging of accepted norms, with processes/systems to support.

Train the managers to understand the importance of the real rather than the espoused culture in nurturing talent.

Provide a 'safe' supportive environment, reward 'hard working' Mavericks, make them feel valued.

Teach people how to learn, not how to be taught.

My boss is a time-management freak, to-do lists, recording of all tasks, achievement lists at the end of the week, forecasting for the following week, doesn't fit with my kind of creative work.

Hierarchies reinforce self-importance and status and can crush creativity, suppress better job design at lowest levels on a slow burn. Kill hierarchies! I have identified two Mavericks in my organization (besides me!) they are both bright, prepared to speak out and express often wacky ideas which others listen to. One thing they both have in common is a creative vocabulary – they will use different language and draw great word pictures to get attention and get their ideas across, eg 'in the information blizzard how do you spot a snowflake?' and describe web communication as 'termite technology'. Both are very IT literate and in senior positions. Neither will get to the very top.

Advice for CEOs

The case study interviewees were asked for one piece of advice that they would give to CEOs. Their common advice to CEOs is to get close to your people, give commitment, follow through, don't give out mixed messages, allow communication to come up through middle management, but actively seek it, don't allow it to be changed and modified by those who do not want others to hear.

Use your people, they are your greatest asset, they are the lifeblood of your organization; much innovation can be generated within, light the candles, encourage the 'speak-up' culture for good or bad. Encourage honest feedback, develop real action from their views, never just take it and do nothing, be seen to respond. Some CEOs find it easier to stick with what is known, rather than attempt to convince long-serving people of the need to change. Some executives are daunted by the size of the task, and the speed of change; some simply hope that if they ignore it, by some miracle the market will change and the problem will go away.

On a positive note, other CEOs are embracing change: Philip Lawler, the Managing Director of Hewlett-Packard in the UK, urges businesses to take more risks to stimulate employee's initiative. For example, at HP's research centre in Bristol, employees are encouraged to spend 10% of their work time developing their own non-work related inventions. Like 3M, the actual time allocated is not as important as the principle. 'When people are set free, invariably it's beneficial' says Lawler.

Innovative organizations do not waste time polishing yesterday's apple instead they are searching for the apple of the future. Be proud of your achievements, share the excellence and move ahead again.

CHAPTER 8

Innovation in the 21st century

Be prepared to discover

One of the fascinating aspects of research into innovation and creativity is the way that different people describe the process. On the one hand people have described how they have been stimulated by music, by scents, by strong visual images and where they have needed the company of others to bounce ideas off and to stimulate them. Alternatively others, when they are in 'flow' (see Chapter 3) may work on their own with a sensation of pleasure, where people feel as if they are floating, they are totally immersed in what they are doing, they forget their worries and often lose a sense of time.

Contrast this with innovation, which in many ways is the application of a logical process and individuals often need dogged determination just to keep going until they find a solution. For some this becomes almost obsessive, but often it is more to do with a belief that something is achievable and they have to keep going until they get it right. Thomas Edison is quoted as saying said 'I haven't failed, I have found 10,000 ways that don't work.' Albert Einstein is attributed with stating 'I think and think for months and years. Ninety-nine times, the conclusion is false. The hundredth time I am right.' They are not alone, James Dyson, a modern-day inventor, describes in his autobiography *Against the Odds* how he made hundreds and thousands of cyclones in the early years of developing his vacuum cleaner:

> 'After hundreds of prototypes, thousands of modifications, and millions of tests, I was in terrible debt, but in love with the dual cyclone.'

It is this ability to keep going that is one of the distinguishing features of the inventor. For some it pays off; Dyson says that by 1997 he had a company with a turnover of £100 million in the UK and had generated sales of more than £1 billion worldwide. He has more recently launched a revolutionary approach to a washing machine.

All the best ideas have already been thought of...

What is interesting about invention is that some describe a successful invention as a solution to a problem, but it can also be about creating something that is a better version of what already exists. In *A Better Mousetrap: A Guide for Innovators*, Bissell and Barker list some of the main pitfalls for inventors, which they summarize as follows:

> 'The invention isn't original
> The invention is original, but nobody wants it
> The invention is good, but not good enough
> The invention is too complicated
> The inventor doesn't know enough
> The inventor runs out of money
> The inventor doesn't think like a businessman
> The inventor tries to sell his idea to the wrong companies
> The inventor is too greedy

The inventor falls into bad or incompetent company
The inventor's motives are suspect.'

They then explore each of the headings and offer helpful advice to inventors about how to take their invention through to market, but they also caution them by saying:

'There is no shortage of inventions. But statistically, only one in a hundred has any merit, and only one in three hundred or so is a potential "winner". No matter how novel, or ingenious it may be, an idea has to be saleable to succeed.'

As a potential inventor you may want to argue with their assessment, but one fact is true – being an inventor is not about just coming up with a good idea.

They said it could not be done!

There will always be those who say it can't be done. Surprisingly, there are also those who appear disinterested even when an invention is proven either to solve a problem or save them money. One of our case studies is an inventor, Graham Rawlinson (see Case Study, Chapter 9), and he has had interesting experiences while inventing:

'Innovation can impact at many different levels in our lives. So do you try to be innovative on the big issues, or for every-day kinds of needs? Well, maybe both!

I think my biggest big idea has been working out how to stop tornadoes hitting towns in the USA. Some big ideas come from realizing that the kind of language people are using to explain something is wrong. If you notice that then you have a good chance of finding some great new ideas from getting the explanation right!

Seeing a tornado on TV and wondering what was happening, I looked up the explanation and heard things which suggested that all these buildings, or cows or whatever were being sucked up into the tornado. This really just did not feel right so I worked through what was going on, asking questions from the experts, trying to get them to see that their explanations just did not match reality. In the end, at a conference in California, I presented my idea to a professional audience of scientists and engineers and they agreed that it should be possible, for not too much money, to stop tornadoes hitting small towns. As a bonus the small town gets free electricity as the energy which would have driven the tornado can now drive a generator. Apparently from the Mid-West alone there could be enough power to solve the USA's electricity problem in a totally green way!

But I have used innovation processes (and mostly I use TRIZ, which stands for the Theory of Inventive Problem Solving) to help me decorate the house, clean the house and so on. An idea that people seem to like a lot is using Cling Film over the tops of your kitchen cupboards (after you have cleaned them properly) and every month or so taking it off and putting a fresh layer down. Probably more environmentally friendly than all the chemicals you use to get that grease off!

So, inventing can be simple and fun, a ten-minute game on simple things, or it can be months of work for something really big! Why not do both?'

The reason why some people struggle with invention is that they do not personally believe that they have the capacity to think of an original idea, but it is important to recognize that it does not have to be totally original, it can be a development of an existing idea. A final comment from Graham, 'It is important to focus on innovation, but it is not necessarily about individuals who may be working on their own in their back shed. There is a huge difference between that and creating something that works.'

What about intellectual property?

Many people's perception of an invention is that it is a physical object, something tangible that can be seen or used – as in a product. However, one of the interesting issues for creative individuals and the new breed of knowledge workers is how to protect intellectual property (IP). In many ways the US is ahead of the UK in this. Increasingly large organizations are recognizing the need to integrate IP into the corporate business strategy and to recognize that this has a value that needs to be quantified. Academic institutions, smaller organizations and sole traders are like inventors waking up to the fact that there is a value in what they have created: it may be a business process, a profiling system or a software programme. As discussed in Chapter 6, the potential sponsor or purchaser for this IP may be a more traditional large organization, because for them there is a real advantage in purchasing something that has already been worked on for some time by a passionate owner.

In *Intellectual Property*, a Business Guide produced by the Corporation of British Industry (CBI) and the international consultancy KPMG, there is a useful article by Eastwood and Zair examining how companies can seek to be proactive about their IP assets. They suggest that there is a range of questions that CEOs should ask themselves: one of the most critical is an analysis of what IP assets exist in the organization, where they are held and how they are protected. They suggest that very few organizations will be able to answer these questions with any degree of certainty.

Recording and protecting what you know

In the case of both invention and intellectual property it is absolutely vital to keep meticulous records of all the stages of development. It is also vital that you protect your idea, or your invention by not disclosing too much, too soon. There are a number of ways that you can protect your innovation through patents, trademarks and assigned copyright. However, one of the major issues is disclosure. You can issue confidentiality agreements and sign non-disclosure documents, but it is important to assess the level of risk you are taking when you start talking about your idea. For the passionate inventor who is excited and enthusiastic about their idea this is the hardest part, particularly if you are talking to a potential investor. The best advice is to be careful, recognize the value of what you have created and seek professional advice where appropriate.

Hope for the future

One of the really important aspects of any form of inventing is remaining positive. In the closing stages of James Dyson's autobiography he laments the demise of the UK manufacturing business, and describes the following:

> 'I could lay some blame with the engineers themselves. They should be more assertive; they should resist being pushed into the role of backroom boys. They tend to be nicer, gentler, more creative people and cannon fodder for the sharp-suited City boys. Their problem, I think, is that in discussion about the future of the company, the accountant can prove his point with historical figures, the salesman with marketing data, but the innovator has no proof. He only has the vision of how the future will be, and you can never prove that.'

He says that he couldn't begin to number the meetings that he had with chairmen, directors and MDs who 'refused to see the value of a bagless vacuum cleaner, or the merits of a hose on the back of an upright. I couldn't prove anything, I could only give them my vision.'

On a more positive note, however, he states that he hopes his story will inspire others to go out and make things, initially for fun, and that if they find something that they love, they go further, make it better and keep hold of their dream, that they doggedly pursue their wildest hopes for the future, and if they keep going…

> 'Britain can again become the kind of country that I thought it was when I read the *Eagle*, marvelled at the Mini and ran at night across bridges built by Isambard Kingdom Brunel, afraid of what might be catching me up from behind. It's a Britain our children have never known and it might be just around the corner.'

We need to keep alive that spirit and enthusiasm. We need to encourage, stimulate and foster the spirit of enterprise as illustrated by entrepreneurs like James Dyson and visionaries like Tim Smit of the ecological Eden Project. We need to provide stimulating and creative environments for our children, where discovery learning does not end in primary schools but continues into adulthood. We need to create in the mind of the youngest child setting out on their first day at school a belief that absolutely anything is possible if you want it enough and are prepared to discover how to make it happen.

CHAPTER 9

Doing it their way – the case studies

As this book has evolved I have met some very special people who are excellent examples of doing it differently. Some would describe themselves as being a Maverick; others might challenge that description of themselves. What they all have in common is personal drive and energy, a commitment to improving things for others, passionate beliefs and enthusiasm.

The case studies are of 12 special people who, through their own passion, commitment and wisdom, are working to inspire others, to give people freedom of choice, to support organizations going through change, to help people accept and understand innovation.

They are very down to earth and approachable and have set themselves personal challenges as they worked towards achieving their goals. They care about the world; they want to help organizations support individuals who may have a different approach to work and life.

I am extremely grateful to each of them for their candour, enthusiasm and willingness to be involved. Their stories are inspiring and I hope will provide you with insight into some of the challenges faced by creative, innovative and imaginative people. I also hope that the wisdom they offer will be of value to those with the influence to make a difference and that future generations of learners, employees and other individuals will benefit from changes in their working, learning and social environments.

Unless otherwise stated, case study details are current as at time of interview (2001).

Ian Banyard: Case Study 1

Ian is a Life Coach and Training Consultant with Epona Associates, a company he runs with his partner providing work-life balance, executive team coaching and development, transformational leadership and personal coaching. Ian has developed a reputation as a leading-edge trainer and personal coach through his extensive experience of Neuro Linguistic Programming (NLP) and Emotional and Spiritual Development. As a corporate member of the UK's Chartered Institute of Personnel and Development and a licensed trainer with the Society of NLP, he brings a new dimension and depth to HR development, change management, sales, marketing and customer service, giving clients a fresh perspective. When not leading the way in creative development programmes, Ian invests his time and energy exploring, learning and enjoying life, or relaxing at home in England's Lake District.

Ian, like a number of these case studies, is an independent and free spirit, but he has worked at achieving that freedom. At school he says he was like many others, he just got through, he wasn't the brightest, or a low achiever, he just learned to survive. He felt school was about a game of remembering. He went to an all boys' school, which he says was a culture shock after being at home with two sisters. He said that he quickly learned how to get on with the school bully, the teachers, even the odd kids who had unusual hobbies, he says one of the most valuable things he learned was how to adapt, particularly if you want to influence others.

He also says that he has a drive which someone once described as a 'polarity response', ie if someone tells him 'it's just not possible!' or 'it just is not done that way!' he feels compelled to go and do it, he feels the need to go in the opposite direction from the majority, preferring to discover a new way. This happened to him at school when his physics teacher told him he wouldn't pass his physics exam: he went out and bought a revision guide and memorized all the diagrams and consequently proved his teacher wrong by gaining a 'C' grade.

The desire to find new ways of doing things and the ability to influence has been an important theme throughout his career, which was what led to his interest in NLP. Ian describes NLP as the study of how we use a combination of our thoughts and feelings to manage and develop ourselves and influence others. Early on in his career Ian realized that NLP provided the missing ingredient to his learning process and the key to enhancing his personal effectiveness.

When he left school Ian recalls in a similar way to Peter Honey (see Case Study 4) that he wasn't really sure what to do, so he applied for a number of jobs but was attracted to one offered by the Post Office which had as part of its induction programme seven weeks' training on the south coast. For Ian it was the opportunity at 18 to be paid to live away from home for seven weeks that attracted him most and so he applied and was accepted. When he returned from the course, however, he realized that his course had not included strategies for motivating himself, building his self-confidence and creating positive relationships with customers and work colleagues. Surrounded by long-serving counter-staff and the regular 'customer from hell', he soon realized that perhaps the job was going to be tougher than he had at first imagined. However, Ian soon found that even in a corporate environment there were choices. By using his ability to try new things and his 'polarity response' to difficult situations, he developed coping strategies and people skills that soon attracted attention, and consequently he was promoted from the counter to working in personnel and recruitment.

He found that he was happiest when taking on roles that were not prescriptive, where he could lose the parts of the role that he was less enthusiastic about and develop other parts that he really wanted to do.

He also worked through the Post Office seizing on the opportunity to do things differently; he found that he survived best with supportive managers who gave him guidance on the overall outcome but allowed him the freedom to work out how to get there. The turning point for Ian was when he realized that the only way that he would do anything different was to focus on his own development; he spent four years working on developing his own internal resources and gaining external qualifications.

Finally, having achieved success at a number of levels, he felt ready to leave. He says that because of the work that he had done on his own personal development he felt ready to go out on his own. He had developed enough self-belief to keep him going and, similar to a number of people in our case studies, he believes that 'something will always turn up'; whatever the difficulty it will always work out somehow in the end.

He too believes in synchronicity, and is a firm believer that if you are heading in the right direction you will get the right guidance, the right connections, the right help. However, he equally believes in the saying that if you are heading in the wrong direction, 'the universe throws pebbles, and if you ignore it, it throws a rock' which will make you think more seriously about what you are trying to do.

He says he is also terrible at going back, he doesn't like to backtrack, he prefers to arch round, or start a different route, whether in life, or in a journey and says that he often discovers the place that he was meant to be by following this philosophy. Equally, by travelling intuitively he often arrives at the right place even though he hasn't asked for directions; this is similar to the way Andy Pellant described his way of travelling (see Case Study 10).

Ian says that the hardest part of being different is having to justify something that is not easy to justify to others who want hard evidence. He says that he often operates intuitively, he challenges himself to check his judgement, or tests it out with others that he trusts, his partner, or people that he has found in his network. He says that they are invaluable and that establishing a network hasn't been easy because there are not that many people who think differently, or who won't just come up with the norm.

He gets frustrated when things don't happen, he says it feels like a natural winter, when everything slows down and stops; there is nothing you can do about it. You may be waiting for a response, some feedback, the outcome of a decision, but you are waiting for others and common sense tells you eventually something will happen; but while you are waiting it is hard to focus on and do the other, more relaxing things you know you could be doing, that you normally don't have time to do. He feels that he should see this time as a blessing, and that in reality at a time when you may feel isolated somewhere someone is talking positively about you.

Ian says that his move to Cumbria, to the lakes, was a lifestyle decision to anchor himself, to create a base, which would help him in his inner direction.

Like many of the people in the case studies, he says he doesn't often recognize something as a risk, but his key to handling risk is not to get caught in a corner, he needs to be able to find alternatives; if something isn't working he will try a different approach. He is most proud of 'doing things my way, setting a different role model for my kids, that I haven't sold my soul.'

He is passionate about helping people to achieve, particularly young people with emotional challenges, and is proud of his involvement with the pioneering work of 'Winston's Wish' (a national support service for bereaved children based in the UK) and the Prince's Trust Volunteers

Scheme where he runs many motivational and confidence-building workshops.

Ian's advice to individuals wanting to do something different in their lives is, 'Don't sell out, explore your options, look for opportunities, start working on yourself, think about how you would like to be. Imagine that you have already achieved what you want to achieve, how does it feel? Act as if you are already there. Believe that you can learn anything quickly and easily, in today's society it is a crucial skill.'

His advice to CEOs is:

'Really try to offer flexibility in employment, very few people want to be working set hours. Think about contracting with people for a set amount of time with a specific task, agree and monitor the outcomes but allow more people freedom in the way that they achieve it. Organizations got more out of me in one day, than a week of clock-watching with this type of arrangement. Allow people to work when they are at their most creative. The best companies operate more like the film business when you are given the script, you assemble the best actors and they are project managed to complete the film, they are then called together to work on another film, but in between times they relax, and have their own time.'

Jonathan Evans: Case Study 2

Jonathan has his own learning design consultancy and numbers among his clients ICL Cyber Skills, the World Health Organization, OnLine Education Ltd (Hong Kong), the National Health Service Executive and a number of colleges in the UK and overseas. In addition to the above, Jonathan has extensive consultancy experience in both the public and private sectors and has worked extensively in India, Hong Kong and Australia.

He is a former member of the Open University's Quality Assurance Advisory Group and was also a founder member of its Health Care Approvals Group.

He lives in Bristol with his wife Angie and three young children, Daniel, Jessica and Harry.

Jonathan grew up in a coal mining town in north Nottinghamshire and went to University in Liverpool in the late 1960s. In the 1970s he taught in inner city schools in Liverpool and in Melbourne, Australia. In 1980 he took his Master's degree in Environmental and Pollution control at the University of Manchester. He subsequently joined the School of Education at the University of Bath where he was engaged in a major distance learning research and development project designed to train offshore oil workers in the techniques of drilling. From there Jonathan worked as an educational designer in a technical and further education college in Australia before returning to the UK in 1985 to become Open Learning Director of Avon Training Agency in Bristol.

In 1990 Jonathan became Learning Design Consultant for the UK National Health Service's Training Division (NHSTD) where he developed work-based, degree and Master's degree programmes in management for health service professionals.

Jonathan would describe himself as a Maverick and can recount several instances when he found himself struggling to fit within a corporate environment. However, since deciding to work for himself he has developed an international lifestyle of balancing home and work which not only allows him to work the way he wants but also to spend more time with his family.

Jonathan describes what he thinks are the origins of his Maverick behaviour:

'I'm sure it all started when I went to grammar school. At primary school, I was leader of the gang, successful academically and a real conformist. From there I went to a 400-year-old school (one of the oldest state schools in the country) which had a rigid, authoritarian regime in which academic excellence was the only thing that counted. I hated the place and its petty rules and began not only to fail spectacularly but also to rebel against the institution. I'm sure my dislike of business uniforms is related to my memories of the school uniform!'

Like Peter Honey (Case Study 4) Jonathan says that two of the most significant experiences occurred when he was 14 and at the bottom of the bottom class. The first was in a conversation with a friend of his brother who had a job as a computer programmer and spoke in glowing terms of his salary which was £1,000 a year (a fabulous sum at that time) and more importantly he had a car and could travel to their nearest city, pointing out to Jonathan that he could only travel locally on the bus.

Jonathan was disinterested at first, but as a teenager, once the social benefits of having a car began to be explained, he then enquired how he could become a computer programmer and was told that he needed 2 'O' levels. Jonathan said he had no idea what being a computer programmer entailed, but the attraction of the freedom promised by the car suddenly gave him a different motivation. About the same time he also remembers playing cricket, he was a keen sportsman and he teased another boy about dropping a catch, the boy turned around and said, 'At least I'm not stupid!' Jonathan says that the two incidents motivated him into taking a different attitude to his studies and he worked hard and began to become much more successful, as a result of which his expectations of his ability changed too. He feels that most people can do whatever they want to do with the right motivation and reward.

Freely admitting that he found employment within some organizations difficult, he described some of the issues for him. One of the main issues is about conformity: throughout his career he says that he rarely fitted a traditional job description. The ways that organizations accommodated this were to encourage him to create his own role;

what was interesting about this approach was that often after Jonathan left they didn't replace him, so having created a role it was often uniquely filled by him. He says another frustration for him was working in risk-averse organizations where he would identify new business opportunities, or ways of making real cost savings only to be told, 'that's not our core business'. Equally, he found it was frustrating having good ideas ignored or turned down because of people's unwillingness to change or to try another way of doing it.

Eventually Jonathan ended up working for himself and ironically as a consultant finds that now organizations are much more receptive to his ideas. He says being self-employed is important to him for a number of reasons. He can work when and where it suits him. His creativity often occurs early in the morning, after a run, at odd hours. He says some of the conventionality of employment really irritates him, having to wear a suit, or a tie. At home he does some of his best thinking working barefoot, in shorts and a T-shirt. One of the organizations that employed him struggled with his wearing of a Dennis the Menace badge. He says humour is a key feature in generating creativity in organizations, as is a culture where people socialize across hierarchical boundaries. Jonathan spent four years working in Australia and he said people were much more relaxed and genuinely happy, which he says is a great stimulus for innovation.

He says some organizations have an almost bullying culture where the very antithesis of a creative environment occurs and the emphasis is on 'don't make a mistake'. In this oppressive culture, no one wants to put their head above the parapet because of the risk of having it shot off.

His most powerful learning experiences took place at Avon Training Agency when he worked with John O'Hara and Dick Willis. He described this organization as being ahead of its time. They involved everyone in weekly half-day sessions, which focused on the basic issue 'How could we do everything we do better?' Everyone in the organization felt they had a voice and, as a result, everyone took responsibility for their actions and reflected on the consequences. People were encouraged to become specialists in their own area. There were no falsely imposed boundaries on their creativity.

He said that as a result the organization got constantly better and its reputation grew. A side effect was that there was a constant churn of staff as other organizations poached people and appointed them to more senior positions. Everyone, however, saw this as a positive thing: staff could see that the success of the organization benefited them and when positions became vacant, the reputation of the organization was such that it always had a very high standard of applicants. Everyone was happy and highly motivated. Other organizations, both national and international, came to visit and to look at the organizational models they had created.

He also believes in the power of charismatic leadership; he said he received his best piece of advice from John O'Hara, 'Go out and screw up, don't worry if it doesn't always work out'. Jonathan believes one of the best ways of developing innovation is to try it out. He believes people and organizations only really develop different ways of doing by active experimentation.

When asked how he manages risk, Jonathan replied, 'I don't!' He says much risk is unquantifiable until you get involved, you can get 'analysis paralysis'. He says that he is easily seduced by the excitement of new opportunities and by doing things differently. He is also proud of the different career opportunities that this has presented, whether working in his early career as a teacher in Liverpool, designing realistic learning materials for people working on oil rigs, or creating sports opportunities for young people in Australia; Jonathan has met learning challenges head on and always come up with innovative and elegant solutions.

His advice to CEOs is:

'Don't expect Mavericks to fit into a standard structure. If you do create a special role for them help them to still feel part of the organization. Encourage all your employees to feel empowered and influential, encourage them to take risks, accept that if they take risks they will sometimes fail, however most people can be far more creative than most organizations allow them to be. Create opportunities for them to get together and to share ideas of how the business could be better, give them the satisfaction of seeing their good ideas put into practice, the response can be electrifying. Leadership is so important, create a conduit of ideas, fuel individual creativity.'

Jonathan thought long and hard about what advice he would give to potential Mavericks, but finally had the following thoughts:

'If you are really unhappy in your organization there are plenty of opportunities outside. However, do try and identify like-minded people in your own organization, develop an ability to get on with others. Find out who the real decision makers are, it is likely that there are several, become more politically astute, recognize how to influence. Identify kindred spirits who have been successful, talk to them. Above all believe in yourself, develop your own motivation.'

Ben and Jonathan Finn: Case Study 3

The Sibelius Group

Ben and Jonathan Finn are twin brothers and co-founders of the innovative Sibelius Group, developer of the world's best-selling music notation software. Its flagship programme, Sibelius, is used by famous composers, students and amateurs across the world. As early as 1995 Ben and Jonathan recognized that the internet could revolutionize the print music industry, so the company set out to integrate internet publishing into its software. The company has now signed deals with major publishing houses in the US and Europe.

The Sibelius Group's headquarters are in Cambridge, UK, with a subsidiary company in San Francisco and offices in London, New York, Nashville and Dallas. The company has over 100,000 customers in 70 countries.

Ben and Jonathan undertook their first business venture as schoolboys. Having invented computer versions of a couple of favourite family board games, they tried to sell their ideas to the games' producers. Both companies were so impressed by the quality of the software that the boys nearly clinched the deal, but in the end in-house teams undercut them. Ben attributes their success as programmers to the amount of time they had to experiment: they didn't have to work too hard to stay at the top of their classes. Without realizing it, they were already displaying the Maverick sides of their natures.

This same natural innovative style led them to develop Sibelius, which they wrote before they had any plans to sell it. Once they realized its full potential, they tried to interest publishing companies in the concept. However, when this didn't work out, they decided that the only way forward was to set up their own business. Although it wasn't easy, they were spurred on by the amount of effort they'd invested in the project and were determined to prove the value of Sibelius to the music industry. After two years of hard work and determination they suddenly found themselves running a significant organization. From just themselves they'd become a company of over 50 with employees in the UK and the US.

The business is still growing, with Ben and Jonathan working long hours to stay ahead of the competition. They also still have lots of other creative ideas, some of which are channelled straight into the business, while others get put into cold storage. Many of these are inspired by their outside interests. Ben's include philosophy, composing and singing, while Jonathan's are roller-blading and travel.

They have some practical advice for other Mavericks:

'We'd be loathe to advise individuals to set up in business on their own just on the basis of a brilliant idea. It's one thing to have the brainwave, but totally different to realize it.

'It's also really hard to get another company to buy into a new idea, because they've their own share of brilliant initiatives. Unfortunately, most have already been patented anyway. But if you're really determined to see it through, proceed cautiously.

'If you get to the point of recruiting others take your time. It's better to run a business under-resourced than to recruit the wrong people. Take your time in the interviewing process and rely on your gut instinct. If you don't feel someone's the right fit don't take them on.'

Ben and Jonathan place considerable importance on being accessible and make time to talk to their teams. Although neither of them particularly enjoy the management aspects of running the business, they work hard to create an environment that is supportive for their staff and listen to all their ideas. To this end they have adopted a flat management style and encourage a relaxed atmosphere, helped by flexible working arrangements and generous holiday allowances.

What advice would they offer to the CEO of a large company about how to foster innovation and creativity?

'As we've grown we've been forced to become more structured and have had to introduce regular and formal meetings. However, we've found that staying in touch with the roots of the company is invaluable, as many of the best ideas can get lost in reporting channels. We've also created a dialogue with our customers by making our email address freely available and logging on to chat to them daily.

'To make sure that we make the most of all the suggestions we receive we've developed a system that helps us to record and evaluate every idea.

That way we won't lose the vital spark that may just revolutionize the business.'

Peter Honey: Case Study 4

Peter Honey is a psychologist and author who, for most of his career, has worked as a management consultant. He is founder of Peter Honey Learning, a small publishing house.

He says that he spent much of his time at secondary school doing woodwork and knitting scarves. One day, when he was about 13, his father announced that he had just obtained a post as a school bursar at a small independent school on the Isle of Man, and as part of his package it was agreed that Peter could attend the school without having to sit the usual entrance exam. So Peter suddenly found himself jettisoned from his woodwork and scarves to a minor public school. For the first term he was very unhappy, everything was different, he found himself having to learn different subjects including Latin, he was bottom of the class in the weekly tests and he hated it.

Then he recalls something quite strange happening: he decided almost overnight that he had had enough of being bottom, he also had become very attracted to the idea of becoming a 'praepositor' (in ordinary language, a prefect), they wore gowns, a special tie and were allowed the supreme privilege of not having their trouser pockets sewn up as the other boys did, and so could walk around with their hands in their pockets. All this appealed to Peter and so he began to focus on getting results and he moved from being bottom of the class to third in the class. He never got any higher, but after that he never looked back, he achieved eight 'O' levels and three 'A' levels and then the time came for him to choose a career.

He had always been good at art and everyone around him, his teachers, his parents, his aunts and uncles, assumed he was going to be an artist and so he left school and went to the local art college to do his foundation year. This is when his second experience of doing something different occurred. He woke up one day and thought to himself, 'Do I really want to be an artist?' He realized that he didn't and so he gave up his course. He was under tremendous pressure from everyone around him who could not understand why he had taken this step – particularly since he had no clear ideas on what else he might do.

As a result of dropping out of his course he was then required to do National Service, which to Peter became a lifeline: it gave him two years of thinking time and breathing space. As a young man he found it an amazing experience, he got a commission and was posted to Singapore and saw active service in Malaya as a 'virgin soldier'. On his return he decided to go to university and read psychology. Having completed his degree he then undertook a Dip.Ed. which he says 'cured me of wanting to teach'. Peter went to a large secondary modern school for his teaching practice, shortly after he arrived there was a major flu epidemic, so with all the teachers off sick he ended up virtually running the school with the headmaster. For two weeks he revelled in the challenge and responsibility and then everyone recovered and he had to go back to being a student, and although the headmaster gave him a glowing report it was not the same, and Peter never pursued a career in teaching.

He decided to follow the more traditional graduate route and wrote off to about 25 companies telling them that they ought to employ him. Very few bothered to respond, but one company who did ask him to attend for interview was the Ford Motor Company and he set off to drive to Dagenham in the UK. Initially when he arrived at Dagenham he really was not sure that he wanted to work there and he almost turned around and drove back, but he decided that he ought to go in, because turning up for the interview meant he could at least claim his expenses.

So with that in mind, he went in to the interview and was very laid back; however within five minutes he began to become very interested in what was on offer. He joined a graduate programme with 15 other graduates and became part of a special project which involved a job evaluation scheme that included interviewing people across the business, some level of negotiation and scoring.

Peter says that it was a great experience and a brilliant way of inducting people into a company, and after 18 months he really understood the company, and there was a tremendous feeling of *esprit de corps* among his fellow graduates. Many years later, he is still in touch with some of the people from the project. However, at the end of the project the group was disbanded and Peter was assigned to a personnel officers role in one of the manufacturing divisions. He found the job mainly administrative with little opportunity for creativity and innovation. He continued in that role for about a year, but he found himself hating it and so eventually he left.

He then joined British Airways as a psychologist for three years, but on 9 May 1969 he decided that he had had enough of corporate life and that he wanted to work for himself. At this time being an independent was much rarer than today, and as a young man with young children and a mortgage he says his parents were ashen with worry – but for him it was exactly the right decision and he has never looked back.

He says that he has never planned his career, but he does believe in synchronicity, not in any mystical way, but there are incidents, happenings which seem like coincidences. He says perhaps we make our own coincidences; he remembers one specific occasion when he ran out of work, it was a glorious summer and so he decided to spend time with his family, and not even think about work. As summer ended he finally decided that he needed to address the work issue, so on the day that his children went back to school, he got up, made himself a cup of tea and decided that he must take the situation seriously and do some aggressive marketing. After a few moments the telephone rang, and he was offered a new project. Delighted he went to make another cup of tea and, before he had done anything else, the phone rang again with the offer of yet another interesting project. By the end of the morning his phone had rung three times and he had enough work to keep him going for quite some considerable time, so he put his shorts back on and went outside and relaxed again. He reflected that 'something always crops up'.

He says that the hardest part of being different is having to be brave, brave enough to back a hunch. He describes a number of situations when he has tried different things with audiences which others might describe as silly, where he has gone out on a limb eg performing a golf trick on a table, or chanting a summary at a conference. He says he never takes risks with people but sometimes he just wants to surprise people by doing things that make the learning more memorable.

When asked how he manages risk, he replies that he manages risk by not consulting with anyone, he always keeps his ideas up his sleeve, because he believes that if he told people what he planned to do they would say, 'don't be silly', so he doesn't talk about it. He says that he is always happy to try things out, even physical things, abseiling, or other outdoor activities. His frustrations are mechanical things, never people. He says he is proud of making complicated things simple, and passionate about writing, painting and learning which has always intrigued him.

Peter's advice for individuals is to 'operate as the quote states, "it is easier to ask for forgiveness than for permission"; there are lots of things that individuals can do, but they often assume that they aren't allowed to do it. I don't believe in people doing dangerous or outrageous things, but I would suggest that they experiment with different ways of doing things. I would say to them "Just do it, till someone tells you to stop"'.

His advice to CEO's in large organizations is:

'Whether you like it or not, you are a trendsetter, people take an unhealthy amount of interest in what you say and do. You need to role model being different, you need to bend over backwards to recognize innovation and creativity and to positively discriminate to counter balance the deadening effect that organizations have on creativity and innovation.'

Will Keith: Case Study 5

Will works in International Sales for a global information company.

As you go through life you meet people who intrigue you, many of the people in these case studies I met through a series of 'happenstances', synchronous events, meetings, someone who is suggested by someone else. I first met Will when he was just about to leave the army and was looking for a job. I was immediately bowled over by his energy; he was like a human power pack ready to fire off in a hundred directions. He wanted a job so much that if I had said there was one in John O'Groats he would have set off marching there and then.

Will feels his background was very privileged: the son of a prep school headmaster who put everything into his children's education. At the time, he says, he thought he was hard done by when he saw the wealth of others around him; with hindsight he feels that he was very lucky and to some extent squandered some of the opportunities given to him.

Will explained 'as a schoolmaster's son one tends to take the course of one or two options, either an industrious achiever, an example to others, go to Oxbridge, or to become rebellious, desperately cheeky and the bane of your parent's life. Unfortunately for my parents and my future I chose the latter!'

He suggests that he was a disaster academically, but that he was learning important lessons about life. When he was nine he was at a very expensive prep school. The father of a friend of his arrived at the school by helicopter. 'He had the audacity to land on the cricket square (I loathed cricket and resented the many tedious hours devoted to it) carrying a briefcase with a gold handle.' Will says at that time and until he left university prematurely at the age of 21 he believed that such events were the result of pure wealth. To a certain extent this was true, but later he realized it was 'power' that was the influence on him. 'Not power in the James Bond baddie sort of way – but power as: "I'm more than just a statistic, more than just another average person". Power in the way that others listen to you and therefore you have influence. I thought what is the point of being on this planet if you aren't making a difference, if you are just a statistic, if you are *somebody*.'

Will says that he is blatantly honest and wears his heart on his sleeve. 'It's not that honesty drives me, but I loathe deviousness and lies drive me mad and I am very good at detecting such behaviour. Humour excites me, I love travelling and solving problems and organizing things. I need to get results.'

Will says he is honest and believes in self-determination with a little luck, luck being the ability to seize an opportunity when it's presented. Permission to be different is not a freedom or a privilege but more of a duty to maximize ability and satisfy ambition.

Long term, Will says that he wants to write, to be a politician and a social commentator. In the meantime he wants to be in a career that he is proud of and that will take him places, but that job can't just be any type of job, he wants to be in the Premier League, fighting and dealing with the best of them in that league. 'I don't want to have to do a second rate job, or anything in life just because I can't get into the best. I will just keep striving until I achieve my goals.'

Will is passionate about waste, 'I am obsessive about waste – not leaving lights on, not wasting paper, not taking bags at the supermarket, recycling rubbish, closing windows. I have enjoyed army life and wish to be of service again, hence my desire to be a politician. I enjoy solving people's problems, both mental and logistic. I love providing information and always pass on to those around me humour and fun, be that making people smile and laughing in shops, or nurturing the passionate arguments of a taxi driver!'

Will is frustrated by sycophantic, egotistical people, lack of honesty, poor short-termist government policy and lack of social responsibility.

He manages risk by employing logical thought, preparation, and questioning, and calculated decision making.

His advice for individuals who are different is:

'Pursue your ambition with rigour, furnish your minds with as much literature and as much comment and advice from people in the know so that your dream may gestate and produce reality. In practice one needs to experience as much as possible about what you want to do. However, following Apollo's creed, "Do nothing to excess", one needs to keep other interests alive to avoid becoming target blind. If all that I focused on was the fact that I wanted to become a politician one day I would lose all the richness of life. Exercise every day, read every day, employ balance and try new experiences.'

His advice to CEOs about how to support people who are different is:

'Give employees rope, explain the goals and allow individuals to get there in their own way. Discuss and exploit their ideas, methods and styles.'

Llorett Kemplen: Case Study 6

Llorett Kemplen (38 at the time of the interview) was born and lives in London. She is married with two sons and runs her training consultancy from home. She has many years' experience in learning and development, and was last employed by The Body Shop International plc as Head of Sales Training. Her clients include high street retailers such as The Littlewoods Organization and financial businesses such as First Direct. Llorett established Communicashone, her training consultancy, in 1997. Focusing on communication, Llorett utilizes her skills as an NLP master practitioner to specialize in trainer training and customer service workshops.

Llorett says that she first realized that she was different when she had a sister and she realized that they were very un-alike, and she says that she enjoyed being different from her. She also says that when she works with others she realizes that she often does have a different perspective. She says that others often label this as 'insight'. She often takes decisions based on intuition and uses an NLP process question 'What would happen if?'

Another difference is that she believes that she doesn't see or put boundaries around her decision making, she is more likely to say 'Why not?' rather than 'why should we?' She says throughout her life she has tended to get on and do something, take the risk and await the consequences – often there have been none.

Llorett says that one of her first inspirations was her father saying to her when she was little, 'Life is too short not to be enjoying yourself'. She has used this advice throughout her career and consequently if something isn't working out she is not afraid to scrap it and start again. She doesn't hang on to things that are not working. However, one of her most enjoyable working experiences was at The Body Shop, and she found herself working for them for seven years whereas previously she had five jobs in as many years. The difference she says was that it was very stimulating, there was a 'suck it and see' mentality where she was free to take decisions. It was liberating, particularly as she was working with a number of other people who had out of the box, off the wall thinking.

In contrast she says now that she has her own business she does the majority of her thinking on her own and as a result finds it quite hard when she has to convince other people that it is the right thing to do. When she is on her own she just does it, but when she has to consider others she is more cautious in how she manages the risk.

Looking back she says that she is very proud of what her team from Body Shop have achieved, she says that it was a special time and as a result of the shared creativity they achieved much more than any one of them could have done on their own. She is also proud of her achievements as a mother and sole trader, as she has never felt very grown up.

She is passionate about learning and seeing people developing, she sponsors and gets involved in coaching an under-eights local football team and enjoys seeing how they have grown and developed.

Her frustrations apart from technology are linked to her not being able to do everything, she says she finds it very hard having to give work away to associates. She also dislikes other people's lack of urgency; she admits to thinking very quickly and finds it hard waiting for other people to make decisions.

When describing her own creativity she says that it is a very special experience and that whether she is on her own, or with others, she feels very light, time passes very quickly and often the creative process takes over. She always tries to keep things simple and connections just seem to come from nowhere. She says she sometimes looks back at things she has written and cannot believe that she wrote it. She says the sensation can be very powerful and she sometimes thinks, 'It's like the box has moved but I haven't lifted it yet.'

Her question to CEOs is:

'Do you listen to the ideas of your employees? Do you allow them to challenge you? Do you encourage them to experiment with their ideas, because the overall risk is potentially quite small, however the impact of not encouraging them to share their ideas can be quite demotivating? How much of a block are your middle management, are they acting like a football wall stopping the good ideas reaching you? Do you really know what talent exists in your workforce?'

Her advice to individuals is:

'Explore your dreams as they really can come true. Identify what is stopping you doing what you want to do. Imagine that you have taken the decision to do something differently, and looking back from there (the future), how did it go? What would happen if you did do it? What would be the outcome? What steps could you take to achieve what you want? Map in words and pictures what your future vision could look like and use it as a stimulus to help you achieve what you want.'

Bill Legg: Case Study 7

Bill is a former Ford of Europe executive; he is now retired but is currently chairman of The Royal Cornwall Children's Hospital Appeal.

Bill realized quite early on in life that he had a different outlook; he was evacuated during the War and spent a long time on his own developing ways of surviving and looking after himself.

When he left school he won a scholarship to Ford and he found himself with different ambitions from many of his colleagues. What he recognized very early on in his career was that he wanted to change things, he did not necessarily want to accept the recognized way of doing things. What he also realized was that big companies are quite protective of themselves; there are many checks and balances and restrictions to stop people doing things differently.

However, what he also realized, the closer he got to senior people, was that they were different but there was something about them that he recognized, and he thought if they can do it so can I. As he described, any big company is effectively run by middle management, which he feels lots of organizations overlook. Although the strategy and policies are set by senior management it is the guys in the middle who are caught between trying to interpret and implement the policies of senior management and persuading those working in the engine-room of the company that it is the right thing to do.

Bill experienced a whole range of management styles during his career, including those managers who didn't explain anything. This prompted him to make up his mind that as he progressed up the corporate ladder he was going to explain why a particular course of action was going to be taken and what the implications of particular actions might be, rather than just give orders. There were times when

Bill felt quite alone, it was not easy to act this way; the easiest way to operate he suggests was to just fall in with everyone else and give the usual response, 'Don't ask me why, that's what management wants just get on and do it!' If you take this approach you discourage people questioning anything, yet we know that senior management, because of their remoteness from day-to-day operations are not always right, they can't possibly be.

So how do you persuade senior management that there is a different way of doing things? Bill says that first you must win their trust, then they are more likely to listen to you and you will be in a better position to persuade them that there might be another way of doing something. It is better not to be too challenging initially, begin by exploring different solutions and taking responsibility for the problem. He says that it wasn't easy, there were times when he wondered to himself 'Why am I doing this?' but he said the eventual reward is the satisfaction of knowing that you have made a difference.

His advice to current CEOs is that you really have got to encourage people to contribute. There should be more management forums, discussions with no pre-conceived agenda, opportunities to ask questions and listen to the responses, to encourage people to ask the difficult questions. He feels that while suggestion schemes can be useful they only really play lip service. He is in no doubt that any CEO or manager is only as good as the people that he or she has working for them. Most companies today don't have staff loyalty, when Bill worked for Ford he acknowledged that they didn't do everything right 'but they did give people scope and encouraged ambition, it did not matter who you were, or where you had started in the business you could achieve anything that you wanted to do, it was important that the company was successful and trail-blazing and I was proud to be part of it for over 39 years. In today's businesses people seem to sometimes lose track of common sense.'

Bill says he is not sure he likes the term Maverick. 'Maverick sounds like a loose cannon, while I am not sure that I would describe myself as a Maverick, I do believe that if you keep doing what you believe is right and you work within the rules nothing is written in stone and you can change things. Keep asking the question "Why?", don't be afraid to ask the awkward questions. If you are being challenging for the right reasons because you passionately believe that things can be done differently then that type of Maverick behaviour is acceptable, but if someone was displaying Maverick behaviour selfishly then I would worry.'

Asked what drives him, Bill responded 'I have always wanted to do my very best, I want to give 100%, if I can't do it well, I don't want to do it, whether it is a dinner party, or anything else. I get tremendous satisfaction out of doing things well. Failing doesn't come into it, I know I am going to do it, I may not do it brilliantly but once I have decided that I am going to do it I will keep going until I have achieved it. I am passionate about life and fair play, I like to see people rewarded. Life is a risk and I won't take on everything but I will accept challenges. It also doesn't mean that just because I take something on it always works, I have been burnt more than a few times, but you learn from the experience, a lot of wisdom comes through learning the hard way! The most important thing is never to make the same mistake twice. When I took over the hospital appeal there were a lot of people who didn't believe that we would raise the necessary money, but we have raised the £1.6 million required and built a dedicated children's unit in just over three years.'

Bill is frustrated by people who are negative, who are apathetic who say it can't be done, people who don't respond and people's lack of drive. When he managed people and they told him how it couldn't be done, he asked them to come back and give him reasons how it could be done. He says 'You would be surprised how often they found a way to overcome the problem.'

Bill's final comment was as follows:

'It is a great pity that Mavericks get frustrated and leave organizations, its bad for them and bad for the company. We should do whatever we can to encourage these people to stay, we do need people who see things differently, these people will see ways around the problem. Equally it's very hard being a Maverick on your own, you do need people around you, you need to be able to enthuse others.'

Sheena Matthews: Case Study 8

Sheena has spent most of her career in organizational change and development. She has worked in the public sector and as a management consultant across all industries. At the time of the interview she was on a contract to the Foreign and Commonwealth Office as Change Manager.

Sheena says that she first thought that she was different when she got to her primary school; she had attended a convent school from when she was three, and then her parents moved and she transferred to the state primary system at six years old. A number of things were different: she was the only one in the class who was doing joined-up writing and she had to get special access to the eleven year olds' library because she was already an avid reader. The school, she says, responded very well but it jolted her initially to realize that she was different from others, more self-confident and independent.

She is the eldest of three children and as she got older she found that being first featured for her in a number of contexts: she became head girl at her grammar school, she was the first in her family to go to university, where she became hall president. When she left and started her career this continued; she was the first female development consultant in the Cabinet Office. 'Intellectually and intuitively I spot patterns. I like working on the edge, or at the tipping point, as new ideas start to work. For example, the power of networking and sharing knowledge, looking at performance through "star" competencies; the importance of organizational and individual ethics, "real leadership"; releasing energy and innovation and organizations that genuinely learn.'

Sheena says that she has been very fortunate in her career and attributes much of her success to being in the right place at the right time. She says some of the challenges are being different without being alien, perceiving what others might not see and working hard at managing that diversity to encourage creativity. In some circumstances she has been treated as an outsider. She recalls a situation many years ago, when she was at her first meeting in one organization. During an early break everyone (all men) left the room; a few minutes later they came back and rather sheepishly told her that normally they make the real decisions in their discussions in the gentlemen's cloakroom. They realized that it was now no longer appropriate to do that. She also said that if you get selected because you are different you will sometimes find yourself excluded from the mainstream, or the inner circle. But that's organizational reality and, whereas others may fit more easily into the mould, you work with this and the difference factor.

When asked about how, as a Maverick, Sheena has fitted into organizations, she said 'By doing things differently, working on change, recognizing where the organization has started from, asking questions and being deliberately counter cultural.'

She says that she has a postcard in her office with a quote by Gertrude Stein, 'Considering how dangerous everything is, nothing is really very frightening'.

She says that she handles risk by just getting on and doing it, and that as she gets older she realizes that worrying about the little things is a waste of time. She tries to encourage others to do things differently and shares in their delight when the sky doesn't fall in. She said that she does not always calculate the odds, she often acts more on intuition and impulse, and will keep doing it if she is enjoying it, and feels confident. However, if she is really out of escape routes, she will just get out, but it has only happened a couple of times. Change sometimes makes people paralyzed like rabbits in headlights and there's no point in just running them over.

She is proud to have played one small part in the overall development of people in lots of different relationships; employees, employers, people who have made a difference, people who have carved out a career, who have left one organization and joined another one and done really well. In terms of business success she says that it is very special when she talks to people in organizations where she has worked and finds that some of the initiatives that she left behind are still working. She is passionate about people and she says all the clichés about people making organizations tick, being the biggest resource and the greatest asset are very true. She is excited by brainpower, other people's passion, and upward spirals of inspiration and innovative ideas. She loves working with charismatic people, getting caught up in something really positive. 'It's like surfing on energy. I am sometimes accused of being too positive, I don't believe you can be too positive, but equally I am not blind to the blocks to change. Others focus on the negatives and difficulties; I like to persuade others to try something different.'

She is frustrated by game playing, hypocrisy, untruthfulness, and 'blind' resistance. 'I expect people to be honest and upfront. The pace of change frustrates me when I've got people who want to get on with it and I have to try and take the whole organization along. I do wonder why others can't see what I can see and seem to want me to go through yesterday's procedures to get to tomorrow.'

She says that her creativity comes with ideas that seem to spring from nowhere, but she captures them on scraps of paper, once a month she reviews them. She also keeps a daybook and again twice a year she looks through them and finds patterns and uses them to identify how she's followed a particular path to reach her current position.

Her advice for CEOs is:

'Be visible and authentic. Connect with the people who work in your organization, believe in all the theories about management by walking about, people do respond, it's about sheer human interest. Encourage a genuine "speak up culture", generate energy and connect with it. The worst thing you can do is kill others' energy. If people do feel valued and recognized at work they will do tremendous things. Don't promote and reward people who are the antithesis of what you are trying to do at times of change. Keep today's and tomorrow's culture in your head at the same time. Model what you want to encourage.'

To individuals she suggests:

'Find like-spirited people and spend time with them, don't get hung up on the fact that you may be different. You will never be accepted by everyone, as long as you feel that you are making a difference just keep going. Be aware of the risks of "going native", by this I mean it is very easy to get sucked into the organization and lose sight of your vision, particularly if there are not enough people who can see what you see. If possible, manage evolution as well as revolution; be bold and try to be patient.'

Stephanie Oerton: Case Study 9

Stephanie Oerton is currently the Talent Development Manager for Freeserve.com on a part-time basis. Her remaining time is spent building up a small consultancy, which she hopes will become a full-time occupation. Stephanie is married with four sons; she loves the challenges their different ages and stages bring. Her interests and passions include: the link between behaviour, learning and psychology, she also enjoys gardening, cycling, reading and of course family.

When asked when she first realized that she was different Stephanie says that it was a slow process of recognition. As a child she says that she noticed that she related to things differently from her brother.

Throughout life she says that her view of the jigsaw was often not the same as her peers. She believed that she could often see a way of co-ordinating and fitting all the pieces together to form the picture whereas sometimes her colleagues could only see the barriers. She says more recently in her career she has tried not to take control of the picture but to help others to see how to fit the last piece.

At school she says that she really struggled to see the relevance of a number of subjects, where she got on well with the teachers she was more successful. She remembers asking questions but not gaining any real answers and she says that she left with a couple of CSEs, yet in her 30s she achieved a degree and now is considering working for herself. The difference is that now she feels that she has learned to learn, and she has made sure that her own children have also been through the adult experience of how to learn.

She has taught them how to use Mind Maps®, she puts stickers over the house reinforcing positive statements about their ability in the subjects where they are less confident. She has shared information with them about their left and right brain and sent them on study skills courses.

Once she left school Stephanie's career was unusual; she spent ten years working in Australia, which she absolutely loved, and she says every organization that she worked for encouraged her to be a Maverick. Fired with energy and enthusiasm she came back to the UK and assumed that she would be treated in the same way. She says that she couldn't have been more wrong and she was so unhappy in her first job that she would have left to become a road-sweeper. The culture was the exact opposite to her employment experiences in Australia, her natural creativity and enthusiasm were completely stifled, and she left very quickly.

By contrast she feels her current company, Freeserve plc, have been fantastic, they have given her tremendous scope and freedom to grow and develop and she feels that they trust her to push the envelope even further than even she may at first have considered.

Stephanie has tremendous personal energy and she says she is often driven by adrenaline to keep going, her optimism often takes her through what she calls her 'lull' period similar to what Ian Banyard (see Case Study 1) describes as the 'natural winter'. These periods provide her with a stimulus to go again. She says that she is naturally very competitive whether it is in her private or working life. She sometimes wakes at 5.00am and works on her ideas and she says that she often has such vivid dreams that she awakes quite exhausted. To recharge she meditates twice a week and goes to the gym as well, which she says is an excellent way of mind clearing.

She is passionate about facilitating other people to develop themselves, and gets very frustrated by people who have the half-empty glass syndrome, who are unwilling to try something different. She says over the years she has learned to avoid people who draw her energy by their negative attitudes.

Like a number of our case studies, Stephanie manages risks in quite a reactive way, she admits that she sometimes handles risk by thinking through how she might need to limit the damage of something she has done. However, she feels that she has usually weighed things up before she makes a decision, and so she normally trusts her judgement.

She says that one of the hardest parts of being different is working with others; she enjoys having other people as a sounding board, but she does also need to spend time on her own thinking things through. She says that one of the positive things that has happened to her is that she has received feedback from a number of people about her ability to get people to do things and her way of bringing people together. She recalls being on holiday in India with her husband when a couple of children came into the hotel and her natural reaction was to take a picture of them with her camera. Suddenly all the family joined in and they got invited to a meal. She was really surprised but her husband pointed out that other people just would not have created such an impact. She says that she has to be careful that she doesn't inflict her energy and overwhelm others.

She says some of her proudest moments are when she gets feedback from others saying that what she has done with them has been of value.

Her advice to CEOs about how to support Mavericks is:

'Give them freedom, encourage them to take risks, remove the blame culture.'

Her advice to Mavericks is:

'Go with your intuition, believe in what you want to do. Just try it; learn from your mistakes.'

Andy Pellant: Case Study 10

Andy operates a portfolio career. He is currently the Personal Development Director of Learn 2 Earn Limited, a leading provider of on-line performance support and personal development e-learning. Andy is also one of the co-founders of The Research Initiative, an organization that specializes in researching the facets of entrepreneurship, enterprise and organizational development. Andy also operates as an executive coach and holds a number of non-executive positions. Andy has trained as a psychotherapist and is particularly interested in the links between personal and organizational development.

Andy is one of the case studies who would describe himself as a Maverick who passionately believes in making a difference, he describes himself as follows:

'I am a son, a father, a parent, a partner and a friend. I am a person who feels and thinks, considers and agonizes over how things could be better. I am skilled in helping people make sense of themselves, their experiences and their world. Sometimes I can even do that for myself.

I am a coach, a developer, a teacher and an orator. I care passionately about people, about their lives and about their capability. I believe that everyone has what it takes to become the person that they always wanted to be. I believe that, unless you are very careful, life is something that happens to you while you are waiting for something better to come along.'

One of the key issues for many of the people in these case studies is recognizing and understanding how to cope with being 'different'. In Andy's case he realized at a comparatively young age, and with some level of horror, that as an only child of a very protective and loving mother he was regarded as 'special and precious' and he desperately wanted to be ordinary.

Like some of the other people in the case studies he found school easy and was regarded as a 'good' student. This applied to a number of aspects of his school life, once he had decided that he wanted to be good at it, he found that he could, so in addition to the academic subjects he was also successful at athletics, rugby and most other sports. He found that he was praised for being mature, and so once he had grasped what was required he could achieve it, hence he progressed from junior to senior school passing the exams with comparative ease. On his first day at secondary school he fainted, and the head boy who carried him out said to him, 'I have a sense that one day you will be head boy and do this for someone else' and it was true, later he did become head boy, and did carry out a new student who fainted in the sunlight on his first day of school.

From a young age Andy has always felt that he has intuitively understood people, and he was desperately upset when his parents protected him when his grandfathers were ill. A protection that extended to never actually saying that they had died, instead they had simply 'gone away'. Even though his mother's family spoke Welsh, he understood enough to survive and to know when he was being talked about. These, then, were two words that summed up his childhood: 'survive and special'.

He left school and went straight to work, he had no desire at that stage to go to university, his major interest was getting on and doing things. His first career interest was in the caring authoritative area, eg Hong Kong Police Force, probation, prison officer, but after careers 'advice' where his options were laid out prescriptively, 'If you don't go to university, then you should go into the forces, banking or insurance', he was persuaded after 'A' levels to go into banking – he was so thrilled that someone wanted him, he decided that he wanted them too.

After 12 months he couldn't stand it any longer so he found himself a job as a salesman with one of the first businesses that were offering a retainer, having got one retainer he then convinced three other companies to also retain him, he was only 19 years old at this stage. Following the petrol crisis the bottom fell out of the plastic industry that he was working in and at 21 he decided that he needed proper training. He got trained in sales and again applied his energies so that he became a very successful salesman.

His sales career continued through to senior management level and the creation of more businesses, eventually selling out to a public company and joining the main board as he went through an 'earn-out'.

During his time as a salesman and as a sales manager Andy began to recognize some of the patterns of behaviour that kept him 'stuck'. He began to try and please his bosses, worked long hours and put on weight. At 30 he was more than 20 stone in weight, was going from Monday to Friday without seeing his young daughter awake and was slipping out of his first marriage.

Just prior to forming the company that went public, Andy began a new relationship and within weeks realized that some of the patterns that had driven him and his new partner together were now beginning to risk breaking them apart. Andy went in search of support and settled on a humanistic therapy centre in north London. Over the next ten years Andy threw himself into self-understanding and discovery. He worked in areas as diverse as relationship skills, anger management, family therapy and sexuality before deciding to focus his learning back into the workplace. The workplace, Andy discovered, is the easiest place to observe people at their best and their worst. Here all the family dynamics are exhibited but there is no family around, so the strategies and techniques rarely work and this leads to huge disappointment and frustration and with that comes the possibility of change.

His drivers are a desire for approval, with an innate sense of competitiveness against himself rather than anyone else. He says that he has a feeling of never being quite good enough, and not having had the approval he desired from his father he recognizes that he can become obsessed with the destination and not take enough time to enjoy the journey. He has overcome this by recognizing the need to talk about the journey, to become articulate about the steps and the distance travelled. He admits to getting frustrated with the small chunk stuff, he likes the big chunks and sometimes ignores the steps on the way in both a journey and life.

He is passionate about fairness, as different from equality, he doesn't believe that everyone should have the same, but that people should have what they need. He tries to treat everyone fairly, but this can mean that he spreads himself too thinly, trying to do everything for everyone who asks, but he has had to close his circle, not to network as much, because he cannot always deliver everything that is asked of him. Although he can manage others he has no desire to do it for any length of time, he says he is not a great delegator, but a great abdicator!

He says that part of being special is the ability to become obsessed and very focused, as a classic introvert he has internal energies to solve problems.

Andy says that one of the hardest parts of being different is that it is possible to conform so that others do not really understand that you are different. He says that he has learned to give himself permission to be different, eg when presenting to groups he allows himself to be passionate, or talking one-to-one he is able to share his wisdom, or be evangelical. In day-to-day business it is not so easy; people are neither ready nor appreciative of it. He says that he wishes he could be slightly crazier. 'People see me as nice, safe, solid; I would prefer it if people saw me as slightly dangerous, unpredictable, likely to say something provocative, to be able to be honest when it is needed most.'

Andy's advice to others is:

'Everyone's "special", is different, make sure that you do enough special things every day, every week to keep in touch with your specialness. If you conform too long, or don't use it, it dissipates. Develop "internal talk" that recognizes that special and isolated don't mean the same thing. You do not need to be lonely to be special.'

He offers the following advice to CEO's of large organizations:

'Stop trying to believe that your power comes from what you know, and recognize that power comes from what you ask. Be remembered for the contact that you had with people, ask difficult questions, ask stupid questions but for God's sake get involved with people. Ask your people what they would do if they were the MD. Spend three hours with a new hire within five days of their joining rather than talking to them as part of a crowd once a year. Create an obsession with nurturing people and diversity. Be extraordinary, it amazes me how CEOs do ordinary things and want to be thought extraordinary.'

When asked how he manages risk, he explained that the things that other people see as risk he doesn't, you can always re-build businesses, if you run out of money you go and find more. He says every problem can be overcome, risk is there to be dealt with rather than avoided. Risk and dangers only become frightening because they are not talked out. This applies not only to work but also in our lives outside work; within relationships, supporting family, illnesses.

He is proudest of the conversations that people have had about him, hearing a year after an event, or a speech, or a counselling session that something that he has said had a major impact on them. He says he is not proud of possessions or achievements, but instead values the fact that people want to work with him, that his kids are well parented, that he can hug his father rather than shake the hand of a millionaire.

His biggest frustrations are bigotry, inactive people who just wait before they take risks, who hide behind bureaucracy, anyone who gives excuses rather than reasons. He passionately believes that anyone who takes on a role as a coach, therapist or counsellor should work through their own issues first. 'Being aware of who you are and your biases is just common sense, unfortunately it isn't always common practice.'

His key influencers are his Uncle John, who gave him a model of how to be generous of spirit, his grandfathers who showed him how to be a gentleman, plus two grandmothers and five aunts who gave him instruction in how to have a conversation.

He still feels held back by his own self doubts, about his own value, ability, lack of knowledge of how to engage in a particular sector, he also fears rejection. However, despite this his aspirations are to be known, recognized and talked about as making a difference.

Graham Rawlinson: Case Study 11

Graham describes himself as follows: 'I teach people simple processes for innovation and occasionally come up with an invention or two.'

Graham says the first time he acknowledged that he might be different was when he was about six. Although the youngest of three children, his mother described him as the one who could always solve problems. Looking back he says he wishes that he could have had more of a childhood.

The ability to solve problems is something that has stayed with him throughout his life. In fact he says one of the most difficult parts of being creative and innovative is that he finds it very hard if someone comes to him with a problem not to help; particularly if you can see a way through. He finds it difficult to turn people away.

School was relatively easy for him and he says provided he kept ahead of what was expected he tended to be able do his own thing. Like Ian Banyard (see Case Study 1) he learnt to choose the right friends and create space for himself.

As a Libran he says balance is very important for him, he tries to maintain a balance between creative and analytical activities. He says he learned at an early age that science doesn't give you the answers. He believes, however, if you identify the outcomes and identify a process you can solve most problems.

He believes creativity is easy and with the right process people can create thousands of ideas. How many of them are workable or useful is more questionable, but he believes he can prove in just a few minutes that everyone has the ability to be creative.

'I say this as it is easy to prove logically. Take any object, describe one feature of that object, now increase the simplicity of that feature or increase the complexity. You can do this with every feature that object has. Take, for example, a marketing campaign: any feature can be taken and changed: make it more local, make it more global, make it vary in time, make it vary in colour, make it vary in pitch, make it vary in frequency etc.'

Like many of the case study respondents he says that if there isn't a big risk he will test the limits, exploring and learning from the experience. Having been an educational psychologist for 13 years he says that this approach also applies to the development of children. It is often those who had enough freedom to experiment and test their boundaries who are better able to survive in later life.

However, he says that if he finds himself in a more high-risk situation he feels that he has a moral and scientific duty to ensure that there is a good measure of analytical activity to work through the logic and test the idea before moving forward. He feels that within organizations it is not enough simply to encourage innovation you need to separate out the big risks from the smaller risks. He says sometimes the analysis may look absolutely right, or alternatively your intuition may suggest that you take a certain course of action. However, relying on either on their own may not be the right thing to do; he believes it is important to keep switching between the two.

Apart from his two sons, one of the things he is most proud of is his experience of writing a television series teaching mathematics to adults. As a concept it was one of the first examples, apart from the Open University, of direct teaching using television. Before he wrote the series he had no experience of writing for television, but through inspiration, logic, timing and pacing he and a colleague created programmes, which despite opposition from purists who said it couldn't be done, were a great success. It was stored in TV archives as a first of its kind and at one stage was the most repeated programme on TV.

Graham is passionate about reality; he is frustrated with the education system because he says there are so many examples of bad practice and there are few attempts to teach kids how to learn for themselves. He has a strong belief in the scientific process, but says, 'We can be confused about what it is that we actually know; there is a reality at different levels. Thinking advances slowly – but 90% of what people say is froth – we must get nearer to the truth.'

His advice for CEOs is:

'First of all be really willing to commit yourself to the job. There are no quick answers; you need to develop your own process for achieving the outcomes. People should create innovative organizations where everything is interconnected and relates to the other parts of the business. It has to fit into that reality. It will take work to get there in a way that is successful for you. It is not about being more creative, but it is about having honest objectives and being dedicated to the outcomes. The easiest company that I have worked with was Coca-Cola, because although they had great ideas they were also very good at getting the job done.'

His advice for individuals is:

'I believe it is about managing and understanding dialogue; not hearing confrontation and avoiding negativity but working on a positive approach, focusing on truth.'

Dr Alan Stanhope: Case Study 12

As a principal of one of South West England's leading centres of further and higher education, Dr Alan Stanhope has had his fair share of challenges during his ten years at Cornwall College; however his achievements have been highly significant. Using his own personal commitment and energy he has steered the college through the achievement of a number of awards, Investor in People, BS 5750/IS0 9000 and is rated as Grade 1 in Quality of Governance. He constantly strives for improvement and is passionate about wanting to give his customers, be they students, the local community or users of the many enterprises in which he is involved, excellent service, and the opportunity to realize their ambitions.

So how do you foster creativity and innovation in an academic institution? Alan attributes part of his success to the very sound business principles to which he adheres. As accounting officer for the college he is ultimately accountable and so has an underpinning discipline of assessing risk in the college and to himself. He does not believe in telling people what to do; he has a strong belief in delegating responsibility. He uses the twin controls of financial and quality systems to encourage his teams to monitor and manage their progress and success. However, once the controls are in place he encourages his teams to form and perform, devolving control to small self-managed teams who respond by setting themselves targets.

His drivers are an in-built desire to succeed, whatever he takes on in life he wants to make it better than what he started with, he likes the stimulation of working with others and he is in anti-retirement mode. He admits to being fairly self-contained and self-motivated. He was brought up in an environment where his parents worked hard, things didn't come that easily, he takes a dim view of people who say 'I'm bored, entertain me'. He believes that what you earn you value, what you are given you value less.

He believes in synchronicity, the meeting of the right people at the right time and his creative mind is able to spot connections and link people together who he believes can offer value to each other.

He has an ability quickly to assimilate information, an invaluable asset in the field of education when it is important to interpret vast documents and assess their relevance and application to the college, or the local community. He likes generating creative and novel solutions to existing problems. He is constantly undertaking environmental scanning, stimulating others, looking for ways of improving the college, or the provision of further and higher education in Cornwall. More than that, he also embodies the spirit of enterprise, having been success-fully involved with a number of start-up businesses within the South West, including the futuristic Eden Project. Tim Smit says of Alan:

'Alan is a highly unusual man in that he is essentially an entrepreneur working within the education system. His courage in investing in things that have a "risk" element such as Eden, in order to influence the future for his students is a quality that is sorely lacking in his peers. Cornwall is extremely lucky to have him.'

By contrast he is frustrated by people who have hidden agendas, the blockers, people who can't cope with ambiguity and slow everything down by going into far too much detail; he is a pace setting manager, he likes to work things through until he can begin to see the solution and then he is only too happy to hand the project on to someone else.

He gives the following advice to budding entrepreneurs:

'Work harder, think outside the box, don't take what you are taught as gospel, be positive, question things, challenge and be prepared to change.'

Asked if he could change one thing about education, he replied:

'Remove incremental pay scales for teachers. This would shift the culture to what you do rather than how long you have taught. Reward quality, we have already adopted this approach and it has made a significant difference.'

CHAPTER 10

Doing it differently – why bother?

So here we are almost at the end, and I still have the same sense of wonder that I had in Chapter 1. What will it take to make a significant difference in enough organizations so that every individual is able to really fulfil their potential? There are, I believe, three important elements:

Leading from the front

First CEOs, executive boards and leaders with power, influence and the ability to instigate real change: ultimately it is within your remit to set the standards, create the climate, persuade the stakeholders of the value of developing individual potential.

To each leader I would ask the following:

1. Do you want recognition as a business leader who was not only visionary, but who also took the time to talk to, show interest in and be with your employees?

2. Do you want to be remembered as someone who came in, picked up the business, and didn't just listen to feedback from your employees, customers and suppliers, but actually worked with them to make it better?

3. Do you want to be the leader who took away the role of controlling manager and replaced it with developing managers as coaches and experienced guides?

4. Do you want to be known as the leader who took away the formality of a uniform that people can hide behind and replaced it with the ownership and responsibility of caring about the business's reputation with your customers and a passion for getting it right?

5. Do you want to be the leader that interviews new employees and tells them that it is not qualifications that matter, but a passion for discovery, a willingness to learn, a love for the product/or service and a caring for others that will gain them a place in your organization?

6. Do you want to be the leader that once a month runs sessions for all your employees when you really talk to them and they can talk to you? Not through stage-managed question and answer sessions, but ones where you actually talk to each other so that they have a real understanding of the commercial viability of the business and how they can help to add value, and you have the opportunity to learn first-hand about the real issues in the company?

7. Do you want to be the leader who supplements this by every day being in the business, talking to your customers, having coffee with your employees, meeting suppliers, being enthusiastic with the media, acknowledging what isn't working, showing that you care about getting it right?

8. Do you want to be the leader who takes community investment seriously, and links with local schools encouraging a realistic understanding of how business works and helping them to make more informed choices about careers?

9. Do you want to be the leader who recognizes the importance of innovation not by using a special group of people, but by encouraging everyone to continually work to improve and sustain excellence in your products and services?

10. Do you want to be the leader who is not intimidated by employee churn, but recognizes that there is a need to understand and develop different patterns of employment that support and acknowledge the different life stages of employees? That can support study leave, encourages employees to travel, to visit other employers, to leave and return, revitalized?

11. Do you recognize the importance of working conditions for employees, their need for space and time to think? That people have different learning styles; some will learn through active experimentation, some through reflection and all will benefit from coaching support?

12. Do you want to be the leader who goes home to your partner, family, or friends and shares the same principles of caring, interest and love, and who knows that what you are building at work is something so precious that in time you will all look back and remember that together you did something very special and you can honestly say 'I really did make a difference'?

If your answer to any of these is 'Yes' then you and your organization need to work together not only to enable you to achieve your full potential, but to enable each individual employee to do so too. Every organization needs to support and encourage all CEOs and organization leaders to lead with charisma and passion as well as good business sense.

The organizational climate

We have an enormous responsibility to future generations to make it better for them; more and more organizations are recognizing the importance of taking community investment seriously. Consumers and employees jaded by organizational politics are focusing more on the importance of values. One of the most critical areas will be overcoming the frustration and apathy of individuals within corporate life.

Every analysis in recent years has shown a growth in self-employment and the setting up of small businesses. Many young people leave school or university with no clear idea of what to do with the rest of their life, we are still not succeeding in creating dynamic links between education and industry.

These very real issues do not just apply to Mavericks, they have serious implications for every socially responsible adult.

- We need to create an organizational climate that respects and supports individual development.
- We need to support and develop managers to coach, motivate and inspire their teams.
- We need to support and encourage all employees in taking responsibility for their own development.
- We need to create an environment where everyone has a voice, people listen to each other, individuals take responsibility, everyone works to make it better.
- We need to ensure that the importance of people's life outside work is respected.
- We need to encourage all employees to make sure that good commercial practices are employed.

- We need to find proactive ways of ensuring that creativity and innovation is fostered and encouraged.
- We need to find ways of recognizing and rewarding all employees for their contribution.

Developing individual freedom

If you know you are different from a young age there is often an accompanying responsibility which asks, 'What do I do about this? If I have knowledge how and when do I share it?' Each individual in an organization has a personal choice: 'Do I buy into this organization and really give of my best, or do I play on the sidelines?' From all the comments in the questionnaires recorded in earlier chapters and in the case studies it is obvious how much common sense and wisdom exists in the minds of employees; and yet how many are able to find a voice that is heard by the right people?

Time and time again we read reports of leaders being surprised of the strength of feeling from individuals about certain issues. The reason for this is often simple, individuals do not have the chance to communicate directly with their leaders, leaders are not available to question and listen and sometimes the organization structure gets in the way of communications as is illustrated in the Maverick fable at the start of this book.

To individuals, whether you think you may be a Maverick or not, I would say the following:

Know yourself

Use profiling, one-to-one discussions, feedback to understand and keep learning about yourself.

Believe in yourself

Develop your own personal brand values, have a clear understanding of what you stand for and how you would want to be remembered. Develop the ability not only to go outside the box, but also to go outside yourself – view your progress objectively.

Recognize what you need from an organization

The environment, the management style, how to achieve win-win. Set yourself goals, both life and work; be prepared to ask for what you want, but also what you are prepared to give to the organization, your team and your community.

Apply influencing and relationship building skills

Being different is tough, the Mavericks that succeed apply other skills, and they create a potent mix of high self-esteem and self-confidence to persuade and influence others.

Have a sensible approach for implementation

Ask for help from others, work as a team, play to each other's strengths, use planning, build in evaluation, but don't shut down too soon on ideas.

Ongoing monitoring and managing of success

Learn from mistakes, learn from successes, recognize and celebrate what you have achieved.

Making a difference

All that remains is for me once again to thank everyone who contributed so willingly and so wisely to this book. Thank you for taking the time to read it. I hope you have found it interesting; whatever role you have in life, you have it within your power to help, assist, coach, lead, motivate, develop or enthuse someone else. As you go through the doors of your organization tomorrow, it's your choice… will you be brave enough to stand up and really make a difference?

Appendix

MANAGING THE MAVERICKS QUESTIONNAIRE

All responses will be non attributable and used only to develop quantifiable and qualitative research data, the results of which will be circulated to all respondents and used in *Managing the Mavericks* book.

1. Thinking back over your learning experiences, how do you prefer to learn?

2. What are the best conditions that help you to be creative/innovative?

3. In an ideal world how do you like to work?
   - environment?
   - hours?
   - work colleagues?
   - management style?
   - employed?
   - self-employed?

4. How much responsibility do you want?

                                         – managing yourself
                                         – managing others
                                         – managing process

5. What are your sources of inspiration?

6. What is the hardest part of being creative?

7. What is the most rewarding part of being creative?

8. What does your organization do that inhibits creativity and innovation?

9. What does your organization do to stimulate creativity and innovation?

10. How would you define a Maverick?

11. What do you think Mavericks want from an organization?

12. If you could change one aspect of organizations that would encourage the nurturing of talent, what would you recommend?

Is there anything else that you would like to add?

Thank you for completing this questionnaire.

Bibliography/Further reading

Belasco, James A (1990), *Teaching the Elephant to Dance: Empowering Change in Your Organization* (Hutchinson Business, London).

Belbin, Meredith B (1981), *Management Teams* (Heinemann, London).

Bennis, W and Biederman, P W (1997), *Organizing Genius* (Nicholas Brealey, London).

Black, Jack (1994), *Mindstore* (Thorsons, London).

Bohm, David and Nichol, Lee (1996), *On Dialogue* (Routledge, London).

Bissell, P and Barker, G (1988), *A Better Mousetrap: A Guide for Innovators* (Wordbase Publications, West Yorkshire).

Buzan, Tony (4th ed., 1995), *Use Your Head* (BBC, London).

Buzan, Tony and Buzan, Barry (1993), *The Mind Map Book* (BBC, London).

CBI in association with KPMG (2001), *Intellectual Property* (CBI, London).

Csikszentmihalyi, Mihaly (1990), *Flow* (Harper & Row, London).

Dyson, J (1998), *Against the Odds, An Autobiography* (Trafalgar Square, London).

De Bono, E (1999), *Six Thinking Hats* (Little Brown & Co, Boston).

Gardner, H (1993), *Frames of Mind* (Basic Books, New York).

Goleman, Daniel (1999), *Working with Emotional Intelligence* (Bloomsbury, London).

Handy, Charles (1994), *The Empty Raincoat* (Hutchinson, London).

Handy, Charles (1995), *Beyond Certainty* (Hutchinson, London).

Heller, Robert (1998), *In Search of European Excellence* (HarperCollins Business, London).

Helmstetter, Shad (1998), *What to Say When You Talk to Yourself* (Cynus).

Jaworski, Joe and Senge, Peter (1998), *Synchronicity: The Inner Path of Leadership* (Berrett-Koehler, San Francisco).

Kanter, Rosabeth M (1983), *The Change Masters* (Allen and Unwin, London).

Kanter, Rosabeth M (1989), *When Giants Learn to Dance* (Simon and Schuster, London).

Kolb, David A, Rubin, I M and McIntyre, J M (4th ed., 1994), *Organizational Psychology, An Experiential Approach to Organizational Behavior* (Prentice-Hall, London).

Kao, John (1996), *Jamming: The Art & Discipline of Business Creativity* (HarperCollins, London).

LeBoeuf, Michael (1976), *Creative Thinking* (Piatkus, London).

McNally, David (1993), *Even Angels Need a Push* (Thorsons, London).

O'Connor, Joseph and Seymour, John (1990), *Introducing NLP Neuro Linguistic Programming* (Mandala, London).

O'Connor, Joseph and Seymour, John (1994), *Training with NLP, Skills for Managers, Trainers and Communicators* (Thorsons, London).

Peters, Tom (1992), *Liberation Management* (Macmillan, London).

Peters, Tom (1997), *The Circle of Innovation* (Hodder & Stoughton, London).

Peters, Tom and Austin, Nancy (1985), *A Passion for Excellence* (Collins, London).

Rawlinson, G (2002), *How to Invent (Almost) Anything* (Spiro Press, London).

Redfield, James and Adrienne, Carol (1995), *The Celestine Prophecy: An Experiential Guide* (Bantam Books, London).

Redfield, James (1998), *The Celestine Vision* (Bantam Books, London).

Ridderstråle, J and Nordstrom, K (2000), *Funky Business* (ft.com London).

Robinson, A and Stern S (1997), *Corporate Creativity* (Berrett-Koehler, San Francisco).

Salovey, P, Mayer, J D and Caruso, D R (1997), 'Emotional Intelligence Meets Traditional Standards for an Intelligence' (unpublished manuscript).

Seldes, George (1983), The Great Quotations (The Citadel Press, Secaucus, New Jersey).

Semler, Ricardo (1993), *Maverick* (Arrow, London).

Senge, Peter M, (1990), *The Fifth Discipline* (Doubleday, New York).

Slater, Robert (1998), *Jack Welch and the GE Way: Management Insights and Leadership Secrets of the Legendary CEO* (McGraw-Hill).

Thorne, K and Machray, A (2000), *World Class Training: Providing Training Excellence* (Kogan Page, London).

Thorne, K and Mackey, D (2nd ed., 2001), *Everything You Ever Needed to Know About Training* (Kogan Page, London).

Thorne, K (2001), *Personal Coaching, Releasing Potential at Work* (Kogan Page, London).

Torrance, P (1995), *Why Fly? A Philosophy of Creativity* (Ablex Publishing, Westport Conn.).